Solar Politics

Theory Redux series
Series editor: Laurent de Sutter

Solar Politics

Oxana Timofeeva

polity

First published in 2022 by Polity Press

Polity Press
65 Bridge Street
Cambridge CB2 1UR, UK

Polity Press
101 Station Landing
Suite 300
Medford, MA 02155, USA

ISBN-13: 978-1-5095-4964-1
ISBN-13: 978-1-5095-4965-8 (pb)

A catalogue record for this book is available from the British Library.

Library of Congress Control Number: 2021942281

Typeset in 12.5 on 15 pt Adobe Garamond
by Cheshire Typesetting Ltd, Cuddington, Cheshire
Printed and bound in Great Britain by TJ Books Ltd, Padstow, Cornwall

For further information on Polity, visit our website:
politybooks.com

Contents

Acknowledgments

I have been doing research on Georges Bataille's writings for quite a while, since I was a student; however, his idea of the general, or, to be more precise, solar economy was never really the focus of my interest until the Spring of 2020, when the beginning of the COVID-19 pandemic bluntly intervened in my research plans.

I have to thank Imre Szeman and Allan Stoekl, whose work led me to believe that the idea of discussing Bataille today in terms of ecology and energy politics is not insane. Further reflections made me desire to write a philosophical essay on the sun, which I thought I would endlessly postpone, but, luckily, I was contacted by Laurent de Sutter, to whom I am thankful for his kind invitation to collaborate in Polity's "Theory Redux" series. I am also grateful to John Thompson and the Polity editorial board for valuable tips regarding the initial project; Jeff Diamanti, Benjamin Noys, and Artemy Magun for their comments and critical remarks; Alexander Klose, Benjamin Steiniger, and the "Beauty of oil" collective for insights; Oleg Kharkhordin for not forgetting the Earth, Alexey Zygmont for encouraging me to carry out research on violence, and the students of the Stasis Center for Philosophy at the European University at St. Petersburg, Andrew Glukhovsky, Alexey Sergienko, and Michail Fedorchenko, for their suggestions. I wish to express my gratitude to my family, and to my beloved husband Andrew Zmeul, with whom I was sharing initial drafts and ideas, for his amusing excurses into the perspectives of future technological developments of human and post-human civilizations. Finally, my thanks are due to the comrade sun, who – even in St. Petersburg, where it is usually a rare guest – was so generous during the months when I was writing this book.

Introduction: Two Suns and the City

In 1979, when I was a year old, my family moved from Siberia to Kazakhstan, where my father found employment with a big construction project. On the shores of the great Balkhash Lake, in the grey steppe slipping into a desert, they had to build a city under the name of Solnechny, which translates from the Russian as Sunny, or the City of Sun. It was supposed to be part of a planned industrial construction – of the South Kazakh power station. The first stage of this massive project consisted in preparing the land for construction works – more specifically, they had to transform a hummocky topography into a plain surface. My father was hired as a shot-firer: his job was to blast the hills. We lodged in a very basic wooden barrack, in a small settlement built for construction workers, without basic food and other supplies, eating the meat of rare saiga antelopes that my father was hunting in the steppe, and fish and water taken from the lake. The scariest residents of the steppe were scorpion-sized solifuges, or sun spiders: it was mistakenly believed there that their bites were lethal. Eventually, the City of Sun was never built, and all the funds for this ambitious project literally went into the sand.

Besides the many localities in the vast spaces of the former Soviet Union and beyond that bear the name "sunny," there are also a number of unbuilt Cities of Sun, for which we never stop to blast out the rocks. They are called utopias: in a long historical tradition, the idea of the possibility of organizing a settlement according to certain rational principles, with the infrastructures designed as perfectly as possible to satisfy human needs and desires and to make their collective life to the fullest extent bright and happy, is associated with the image of our central star. From Plato's *Republic*, to the modern-day Solarpunk speculative fiction and the prospects for more ecological sustainable economies provided by renewed energy expansion, the spirit of solarity frames the most elevated political projects for the future.

The paramount importance of the sun for our utopian imaginations is accounted for by its radiation, which is the ultimate source of all life on Earth. That is why in antiquity it was worshipped as a demiurge, or one of the supreme gods: Ra in Egypt, Tonatiuh in Aztec culture, Surya in Hinduism, Sol Invictus in the Roman Empire are just a few names for this multifaced deity. All over the place, there were numerous gods of the sun, of both genders, corresponding to different seasons of the year and different times of the day. Just like Helios in Ancient Greece, the Slavic early deity of the sun rides the sky in a golden chariot carrying with him a bright fire shield. His name is Dazhbog, or giving-god. He gives everything: light, warmth, and wealth. In one version, he is getting old and dies every evening, but is reborn every morning; in the other, he dies in December, and then is reborn after the winter solstice. Our ancestors welcomed their sun gods returning from the darkness of the night. For them, the radiant circle observable in the sky was literally the body of god, whose rays enabled each new day.

Remaining in general faithful to the broad tradition of sun worship, Plato, the author of the reputedly first political utopia, introduces new content to this mythic worldview. In Book VI of the *Republic*, Socrates explains to his interlocutor, Glaucon, that there are actually two suns: the one that we see and the one that we don't see. The sun that we see reigns in the world of visible objects. It is itself a visible object, which differs, however, from all other objects in that it also presents the source of their visibility. Why do we see objects? First, because we have eyes. Second, because there is light. Third, because there is sun, that dispenses light. Socrates addresses the sun as one "of the gods in heavens," whose gift of light "enables our sight to see so excellently well, and makes visible objects appear."[1] The same holds for the intellectual world: just as the faculty of sight comprises the dialectics of the sun, the light, and the eyes, the faculty of thought aggregates the highest good, truth, and knowledge. Moreover, just as the physical sun gives to the objects of the visible world "not only the faculty of being seen, but also their vitality, growth, and nutriment," so the spiritual sun gives to the objects of knowledge "not only the gift of being known," but also "a real and essential existence."[2]

Book VII of the *Republic* famously begins with the primal scene of philosophy which can be traced back to the age of cave dwelling. A group of people is confined in a cavern that most notably resembles a cinema theater. They are shackled and can only sit still and look at the wall in front of them, where they see the shadows of what is going on above and behind their backs. There is a fire there, and a roadway nearby with some other people who carry with them figures of men, animals, and other items. Socrates suggests that the people in the cavern who take the shadows to be real things are we ourselves. The one who manages to unchain themself and leave the cavern will see the true sun "as it is in itself in its own territory," as well as the true world exposed to its light. If this person returns to the cave and tries to describe what he saw on the outside, fellow prisoners, accustomed to the darkness of their chamber, will not believe him, and might even try to kill him. As if soothsaying his own death in Athens prison, Socrates invites us to compare the first, visible world, to the cavern, the light of the physical sun to the fire, the reflections of which we see on the screen of shadows, and the upper world outside to the intellectual region of the highest good discovered by the soul.[3]

Besides the dialectic of visible and invisible suns, there is another novelty introduced by Plato in these fragments, which I find extremely important. Namely, for Socrates, the sun is not an adorable thing out there in the sky. Instead of treating it as an external object, he suggests that there are solar elements within humans themselves – like the eye and sight for the physical sun, and knowledge and reason for the spiritual one. Without being identical to the sun, a human eye bears resemblance to it. We can look at this object and see it because in certain aspects we are akin to it. The sun and the eye communicate as if they are looking into each other through the layers of things encompassed by light, and the one reflects the other. A dark pupil in the center of the human eye is surrounded by a colored iris. If we try to look at the sun during the day, we can see that it, too, has a kind of pupil, which is dark, and a bright "iris" that glances from behind it. Just like the human eye, the eye of god has therefore a kind of blind spot at its very center. It is as if the sensual sun was that dark pupil that obscured from us the divine radiance of the iris of truth.

The doubling of the sun in Plato's *Republic* is tricky: it turns out that we cannot see the true sun, which is the highest good, because it is shielded from us by its representative in the sensual world. We are therefore not only endowed with vision by the sun that we see, but coincidently blinded by it. The greatness of Socrates is that behind the visible sun he discerns the invisible, and praises both. As Marsilio Ficino comments in his *Book of the Sun* (1494):

When he was in military service Socrates often used to stand in amazement watching the rising Sun, motionless, his eyes fixed like a statue, to greet the return of the heavenly body. The Platonists, influenced by these and similar signs, would perhaps say that Socrates, inspired since boyhood by a Phoeboean daemon, was accustomed to venerate the Sun above all, and for the same reason was judged by the oracle of Apollo to be the wisest of all the Greeks. I will omit at present a discussion about whether the daemon of Socrates was particularly a genius or an angel – but I certainly would dare to affirm that Socrates in his state of ecstasy had admired not just the visible Sun, but its other, hidden aspect.[4]

In Ficino's interpretation, the sun adored by Socrates not only duplicates, but triplicates: it embodies the idea of the Christian trinity fantastically interlaced with Neoplatonism, Hermetic tradition, astrology, and renaissance magic. Taking as a starting point Plato's comparison of god and the sun, he makes subsequent parallels: on a downward spiral, god dispenses goodness and love, just as the sun dispenses light and warmth. Note that all these things can be understood as different kinds of energy, which both the god and the physical sun generously distribute around the world. Ficino insists on the hierarchical relation between the god and the physical sun: one shouldn't worship the sun as the author of all things because it is in fact only a shadow of the God who is the fundamental creator. Yes, the sun shines brightly, but the light it spreads, according to Ficino, is not even fully its own. The sunlight as such, according to its basic settings, is obscure, as are other celestial bodies that emit their own natural light, which is not that bright. The excessive shine that radiates from the sun is, according to Ficino, a gift that it receives from god: "Indeed the Sun offers that innate light which is somewhat obscure, then immediately another light most evident to the eyes like a visible image of divine intelligence and infinite goodness."[5]

A tendency to portray the two suns as God and his material substitute is further developed by another renaissance thinker and perhaps the most famous writer of the solar utopian tradition, Tommaso Campanella, who, in *The City of the Sun* (1602), describes the religion and the rites of the residents of the ideal state:

The sun and the stars they, so to speak, regard as the living representatives and signs of God, as the temples and holy living altars, and they honor but do not worship them. Beyond all other things they venerate the sun, but they consider no created thing worthy the adoration of worship . . . They contemplate and know God under the image of the Sun, and they call it the sign of God, His face and living image, by means of which light, heat, life, and the making of all things good and bad proceed. Therefore they have built an altar like to the sun in shape, and the priests praise God in the sun and in the stars, as it were His altars, and in the heavens,

His temple as it were; and they pray to good angels, who are, so to speak, the intercessors living in the stars, their strong abodes. For God long since set signs of their beauty in heaven, and of His glory in the sun.[6]

By the end of the book Campanella goes as far as claiming that the sensual sun, whose light Ficino called "obscure," is actually not even good, as God is, but malevolent, for it "strives to burn up the Earth," whereas "God guides the battle to great issues."[7] This implies that the ultra-rational organization of the city (which today reads as overregulation and total control) must reckon with the brutality and explosiveness of the sun, rather than seeking inspiration from its goodness.

Now let me scroll up: in Nick Land's book *The Thirst for Annihilation* (1992), dedicated to Georges Bataille, the two suns are not visible and invisible, or sensual and spiritual, but simply black and white:

A white sun is congealed from patches of light, floating ephemerally at the edge of blindness. This is the illuminating sun, giving what we can keep, the sun whose outpourings are acquired by the body as nutrition, and by the eye as (assimilable) sensation. Plato's sun is of this kind; a distilled sun, a sun which is the very essence of purity, the metaphor of beauty, truth, and goodness. Throughout the cold months, when nature seems to wither and retreat, one awaits the return of this sun in its full radiance. The bounty of the autumn seems to pay homage to it, as the ancients also did.[8]

Against this tradition, the author points to another sun, "the deeper one, dark and contagious."[9] What Plato's main character, Socrates, disregards, according to Land, is the accursed, destructive aspect of the black sun. This aspect was stressed by Bataille, who sketched his own theory of the two suns in the 1930s. Thus, in his short essay "Rotten Sun" (1930), he distinguishes between a sublime sun of mind, on the one hand, and a "rotten" sun of madness and unheard-of violence on the other. The first sun, "confused with the notion of the noon," exists as an abstract object "from the human point of view," whereas the second points to ancient bloody cults and rituals of sacrifice. Bataille recalls the myth of Icarus that "clearly splits the sun in two – the one that was shining at the moment of Icarus's elevation, and the one that melted the wax, causing failure and a screaming fall when Icarus got too close."[10]

Note that between the two suns of Plato, Ficino, and Campanella, on the one hand, and Bataille, on the other, there is a long tradition of praising the black sun in alchemic and occult doctrines. I daresay that this tradition is not so disconnected from Plato's solar metaphysics, dismissed by Land, but rather historically derives from it – through Neoplatonism, Gnosticism, Hermeticism, and other esoteric influences from antiquity, Renaissance culture, and Romanticism. Bataille adopted the symbol of the black sun from Christian mystics before it was appropriated by neo-Nazism, modern paganism, and other contemporary esoteric movements.[11] While Land's interpretation comes later, and his own philosophy of the Dark Enlightenment can be interpreted as part of these recent developments, the tendency of portraying Bataille as an oracle of reaction, dressed in black, is wrong, and must be opposed by another vision of Platonism, which does not coincide with Land's caricatural image of praising exclusively the "distilled" white sun.

Taking off the table the modern desire to rebel against ancient philosophical authorities and the allergy to hierarchizing categories – like the highest good – I invite you to focus on the dialectical aspect of Plato's thought, which might just happen to stay not that far from the dark side of the sun as addressed by Bataille. Think of a line from La Rochefoucauld: "The eye can outstare neither the sun, nor death"; Bataille quotes this in *My Mother*, where he also states that death is "no less divine than the sun."[12] And yet we keep looking at it, and the divine eye of the sun keeps looking at us, although – as Bataille intimates particularly in "The Story of the Eye" – it is blind. If we assume that Bataille and Socrates praise the same sun, then what is really demonic in Socrates' daemon is an insinuation that we always already connected to its darkness through the light, which is all around. We bear it in our eyes. Dialectically speaking, we do not really choose between black and white; in accepting the one, we get both together. The color shifts from black to white and back depending on the light refraction angle, when in the mirror of the sun we relate to the form and matter of sovereignty which suggests itself as the principle of political communities. It is this principle that Land attacks in the first place: "For there is still something

Promethean about Socrates; an attempt to extract power from the sun."[13]

What does this mean – to extract power from the sun? Through the lens of political theology, the sun represents the source of authority, and equates not only to god, but also to earthly sovereigns, like Louis XIV – *le Roi Soleil* – in France or Vladimir, the Fair Sun, in Russia. The solar circle thus becomes one of the signs of supremacy accredited by god to the one on the top of the social pyramid. Through the lens of economics, the sun is literally a fuel, a source of energy that can be extracted, converted, consumed and stored. The sun of theology is a master at whose brilliance everyone must look delightedly, whereas the sun of economics is instead exploited or even enslaved, as is every natural resource in what we call the age of Anthropocene, when planets and stars are no longer considered gods. Both perspectives, indeed, refer to the Promethean myth alluded to by Land, in which the figure of the sun is offered as an answer in two senses to the question "How to build an ideal city?" First, it presents the model of the good that gives the light of knowledge and allows selected people to govern a society, presumably in the best possible way. Second, it appears as the disposable resource of an infinite pure energy in which today's proponents of green capitalism place their hopes.

Does this mean that we must simply abandon the Promethean tradition – which begins by venerating the sun, but gradually substitutes it with god, king, emperor, etc. – or replace it with some new metaphysics, deriving, for instance, from worshipping Gaia or chthonic cults? Although this trend is explicit in contemporary theoretical work, my idea is different. I imagine that solar tradition can overcome itself from within, by its own means. In other words, the principle of solarity – which does not separate from, but unites Bataille with Plato, Ficino, Campanella, and many other authors submitting their own proposals for the great project of City of the Sun – from the very beginning contains in itself the grain of politics that I would call solar, and which can develop into an antidote to such Promethean tendencies as extractivism and the abuse of power. Solar politics is a pathway between these Scylla and Charybdis. In what follows, I will try to approach it through the set of reflections inspired by my reading of Bataille in a virtual dialogue with other writers on solarity, politics, and violence in our times of political, ecological, and social mess, against the background of neoliberal capitalism, the COVID-19 pandemic, and anthropogenic climate change.

Bataille was an untimely thinker. Definitely not an academic philosopher, he developed conceptions that were too radical to be included in the official theoretical canon. In an age of rising fascist mobilization, he was trying to reappropriate notions of the sacred, violence, and sovereignty, and make them work against fascism. Militantly unsystematic, he did not respect disciplinary borders: in his writings, anthropology, political economy, philosophical ontology, psychoanalysis, literary and art criticism intertwine at maximum speed. One of the first to do so in Europe, Bataille began to articulate a connection between economy and ecology, and to reflect on planetary processes, which human beings cannot really estimate, and of which they are nevertheless a part. Bataille's earlier conception of base materialism that considers heterogeneous matter as analogous to the Freudian unconscious and his later theories of nature and society throw fresh light on environmental issues that are extensively discussed today. Bataille's theory of the general economy suggests new ways of creating a utopia based on the visions of the sun in its striking bifurcation.

In *The Solar Anus* (1931) the sun is listed together with coitus, cadavers, or obscurity, among the things that human eyes cannot tolerate. Here, Bataille's cosmology is presented in a very condensed fashion: the essay draws a picture of a dynamic and decentered universe where each thing "is the parody of another, or is the same thing in a deceptive form."[14] Each thing can be equally proclaimed as the principle of all things, and is dragged into the two primary motions that transform into each other – "rotation and sexual movement, whose combination is expressed by the locomotive's wheels and pistons."[15] The circulation of planetary and cosmic energies finds its expression in a seemingly impossible, parodic unity of opposites.[16] Parody is the principle of Bataille's base materialism, which inscribes solar bifurcation at the junction of eroticism, ontology, politics, and epistemology. Stripped of its metaphysical mask of the supreme good, parodied by all kinds of erections (plants, trees, animal bodies) and involved in a constant movement of the "polymorphous and organic coitus"[17] with the Earth, Bataille's sun directs toward it its "luminous violence," whose perfect image is a volcano.

Associating the image of the sun with violence features as a constant theme of Bataille's writings. Sometimes he gives to it a sense that – with certain reservations – one can define as "positive," for he sides with the violence of the sun which runs wild and identifies with the source of this violence – although the word "positive" does not really fit here, because Bataille is a philosopher of negativity, a radical Hegelian, as it were. So, to be more precise, he sides with the negative of the sun, which is, in his perspective, the site of violence. What kind of violence does he mean? How can the sun or any other nonhuman thing ever be violent? What is the place of violence within the framework of the discussion of a possible solar politics? Before touching upon these questions, I will introduce a way of conceptualizing violence beyond commonplace ideas that are more or less familiar to all of us from the contexts of contemporary life and theory.

I

Two Kinds of Violence

The word "violence" serves as an inflating political currency that can be returned as change for all kinds of symbolic transactions. Coming to ordinary language from public politics and the mass media, it applies to actions and affectations of different degrees of brutality, from terrorism to the violation of someone's privacy and psychological autonomy. Police violence; sexual, physical, and emotional violence; war; gender, domestic, ethnic, and racial violence: all become universal elements of social and private lives, designating either situations that escalate and run out of control, or, on the contrary, those where there is too much control. Anthropogenic factors of climate change and mass extinction can also be discussed in terms of violence: an ecological worldview suggests an image of the human as a sum of technology, as violating the Earth, and of the extractive economy treating it as a collection of usable resources. After all, any kind of activity or inactivity can be qualified as violence over something or somebody. I do violence to myself, too, even by making myself write this book.

Given the variety of word usages, there are general tendencies in thoughts about violence today. First, it is definitely a subject of moral condemnation; second, the discourse of violence penetrates all spheres of social life to such an extent that it becomes hard to find anything that wouldn't fall under this label. There is a moral ban on it: violence is evil. It must be exposed and denounced, precluded, stopped, eliminated, minimized, prevented, or punished. With some exceptions, cultural experiences of modern Western societies are framed by highly developed humanistic values. Addressing violence in some positive context therefore seems to go against common sense.

At the same time, the fact that commonsensical judgments comply with moral evaluations does not automatically make them true. Moreover, truth in the philosophical sense may well confront, directly or indirectly, such judgments and evaluations recognized as doxas, dogmas, ideologies, or nonsense. Thus, in the *Phenomenology of Spirit*, Hegel emphasizes that good and evil, in their actualization, converge into each other: virtue is a form of consciousness that acts in the name of abstract good and struggles against the way of the world without realizing that it is itself a part of that great mess that it labels as evil.[1] Inviting us to reevaluate all values, Nietzsche, in turn, pushes philosophy beyond good and evil and displays violence at the origins of all morals.[2] Both Hegel and Nietzsche uncover, in their own way, the hypocrisy and double standards of moralism and suggest alternative ethics that derives from the multidimensionality of the life of Spirit (Hegel) or body (Nietzsche). If Hegel ironically, but gently, turns inside out all evidence of common sense, Nietzsche demolishes it without remorse.

Later, Marxist and leftist tradition radicalizes these antidogmatic tendencies and inscribes the genealogy of moral categories within the history of class struggles. Taking the side of the poor, the wretched, and the oppressed, this tradition is an affront to public morality, which conveys the interests of the ruling classes and privileged groups and represents as good the violence that they commit. It is precisely in the framework of this leftist critic that a very specific apology for violence emerges, but this is not an apology of the violence of the state, of the police, or, generally, of the strongest. What is at stake is not the abuses of power disguised as a common good, but a violent restoration of justice, which is supposed to put an end to social oppression. It is not the field of morality, but a political perspective that generates the new common sense of revolutionary violence, the justifiability of which is debated with regards to historical precedents, from the Paris commune to the recent Black Lives Matter and other popular movements.

Negation of negation

In the twentieth century some bright intellectuals dared to speak up about forms of emancipatory violence – among them, Georges Sorel, Walter Benjamin, and Frantz Fanon. There are grounds for believing, with some reservations, that Bataille too belongs in this category, although his theory of violence falls out of the general line. Here I would like to touch upon these grounds, to juxtapose the conceptions of these thinkers, to expand on the specificities of Bataille's position, and to provide an argument for its relevancy.

There are at least two moments where, on the level of the formal structure, theories of violence, developed by Sorel, Benjamin, Fanon, and Bataille, do have something in common in spite of serious differences. First, there is an idea that there are two antagonistic types of violence. The true violence (Sorel), the divine violence (Benjamin), the absolute violence (Fanon), and the sacred violence (Bataille) are opposed to the actual existing system of legitimate violence, upon which old, exploitative, colonial, or profane regimes of power are based. Sorel opposes a supreme proletarian violence of the general strike to the brutal violence of the capitalist state system; Benjamin introduces divine, or revolutionary, violence contesting the violence of the law; Fanon formulates the idea of the resistance of colonized people that becomes even more violent and brutal than the colonial regime against which it struggles.

Second, there is an explicit asymmetry between these two types of violence. The second type –

upright, rebellious, emancipatory, or redemptive – emerges as a response to the violence of the first type, or simply oppression. However, the violence of the oppressed is not a mere fight back, in which case the opposing sides as variables were simply switching places while the entire formula remained the same. It does not equate and does not mirror the actual existing violence that provoked it, and is not translatable to its language, but exceeds it and thus moves to some new level, or plain of possibilities – thus opening up its utopian dimension.

These two moments constitute a dialectical structure of the double negation. The point is not that we run into a brick wall, but that emancipatory violence corresponds to the negation of negation: for instance, police violence negates personal liberty, while the violence of protesters against the police, by negating this negation, affirms true liberty, which previously existed only in the form of an abstract idea, and now became real. Thus, during protests in Moscow against fake elections in August 2019 a number of people were convicted on charges of civil disorder and violence against the police. What they did were actually minor things like throwing an empty paper coffee cup or a plastic bottle in the direction of the group of policemen that were striking people with batons. This gesture seems so inoffensive and incommensurate: what is a weightless paper cup or a plastic bottle against the police truncheon? And yet, according to law enforcement agencies, these gestures were assuredly categorized as violence. Why? Because this was liberty at work. Suddenly, the truth of deliberate action makes the paper cup weigh more than the truncheon. The violence of the police is not absolute; there can be always a response to it, and this response differs from the oppressive act that provoked it.

Indeed, theories, discussed here, emerged from dissimilar historical contexts, and the authors had completely different examples in mind, inscribing distinctions between two kinds of violence in their own larger projects: Sorel in anarcho-syndicalism, Benjamin in political theology, Fanon in decolonization, and Bataille in the general economy. However, a kind of structural homology makes it possible to introduce these theories into a conversation, which resonates in the spirit of today's life. Among contemporary philosophers, the one who dares to continue this tradition is Slavoj Žižek, according to whom the two kinds of violence are objective and subjective.[3] Subjective violence includes the most visible things, such as crimes, whereas the first type, objective violence, is invisible, normalized, and itself divides into two kinds – symbolic (the violence of language, or symbolic order) and systemic (the violence of capitalism). It is not tolerance, but the struggle against this violence that unites people and gives them a sense of solidarity. Paradoxically, this second kind of violence is driven by the negativity of love. As Žižek states in the concluding chapter of his book on violence, commenting on Benjamin: "*The domain of pure violence*, the domain outside law (legal power), the domain of the violence which is neither law-founding nor law-sustaining, is the domain of love."[4]

General strike

Sorel's *Reflections on Violence* is one of the major references in any substantial theoretical discussion on the topic. In this book the acts of violence are embedded in the politics of class: "These acts can only have historical value if they are *the brutal and clear expression of class struggle.*"[5] Sorel describes class struggle in Marxist terms, as a revolutionary movement of the proletariat against the bourgeoisie; the latter always prefers peace, which means conservation of the status quo. He makes a clear distinction between the two terms "force" and "violence," or, to be more precise, "between bourgeois force and proletarian violence."[6] What I called "violence of the first type," such as violence of the state or the police, is, for Sorel, not really violence, but force, the role of which is "to impose a certain social order."[7] The state and its repressive apparatuses – the army, the police – operate through the regular use of force. In contrast, true violence can only be of the second type; it is a creative longing that tends to destroy the dominant order and actualizes the will of the people. Sorel's idea for revolutionary violence is the proletarian general strike: contrary to the force that is used by the state for maintaining civil order and the illusion of social unity, true violence escalates class antagonism without bloodshed. Revolutionary violence is thus asymmetrical to the force that is available to a certain minority in order to retain power. The violent aspect of the general proletarian strike displays itself when it stops the overall process of production and therefore puts a break on the machine of the capitalist state.

History provides many examples of general strikes as extremely powerful instruments in emancipatory political struggles; among the most recent were the strikes led by the Yellow Vests Movement that begun in France in October 2018, or the nationwide strike in Belarus in October 2020, which was part of the protests against the repressive regime of Alexander Lukashenko. These and other such movements did not succeed in overturning the state, and yet history teaches us that a general strike can lead to political regime change. This happened, for instance, in my city, St. Petersburg, in 1905, when a mass strike movement resulted in the First Russian Revolution, followed by the establishment of the Parliament (Duma), a constitution, and a multiparty system. These events did not change the overall class composition of society; they were just the beginning of the avalanche-like processes. In January 1917, Lenin gave a lecture where he emphasized the historical significance of the 1905 Revolution: "The Russian revolution was the first, though certainly not the last, great revolution in history in which the mass political strike played an extraordinarily important part."[8] However, according to Lenin – who argues about it with syndicalists – the general strike alone does not prove to be sufficient and, as he claimed in 1906, "must be regarded not so much as an independent means of struggle as an auxiliary means in relation to insurrection."[9] The peaceful general strike cannot demolish the state without the next step, which must be an armed uprising. Apparently, Lenin knew what he was talking about. In February 1917, the general strike morphed into another bourgeois-democratic revolution: the workers' movement was joined by the armed forces, and the monarchy was overthrown. The struggle continued, and in a few months the October socialist revolution transformed the former Russian Empire into the proletarian Republic of the Soviets. *Reflections on Violence* was written in 1906, shortly after the First Russian Revolution. What happened in 1917 inspired Sorel to enlarge his statement: in 1919, he added an appendix – "In Defense of Lenin" – to the fourth edition of the book, in which he expressed his admiration for the Bolshevik leader.

It is important to note that historical strikes are not general strikes in Sorel's sense. He discusses the experience of political strikes and points out that, in contrast to them, the general strike must not limit itself to the satisfaction of some actual demands, such us wage increases or a reduction in working hours. Instead, it must aim to demolish the existing system of power relations as such – that is, to demolish the state. It cannot achieve its goals within the existing regime, but must put an end to it. In this sense, the general strike is *unlimited*, and, in Sorel's terms, it is a *myth*. This does not dismiss, however, the sense of the general strike. On the contrary, "it is the myth in its entirety which is alone important."[10] It gives people a perfect image of what they are struggling for. The advantage of the myth is that it releases a powerful positive charge and is capable of mobilizing an energy necessary for emancipatory mass action:

Even supposing the revolutionaries to have been wholly and entirely deluded in setting up this imaginary picture of the general strike, this picture may yet have been, in the course of the preparation of the revolution, a great element of strength if it had embraced all the aspirations of socialism and if it had given to the whole body of revolutionary thought a precision and a rigidity which no other method of thought could have given.[11]

The proletarian general strike as a universal act of civil disobedience presents a pure insurrection that places myth above the rationality of pragmatic goals and gives the integrity of sense to the historical being of the people. The most problematic aspect of this mythic turn is that it made Sorel's theory appropriable by fascists. Radical theories of this kind are always at risk of being misused or pushed in a wrong direction. However, this doesn't eliminate their initial progressive insight. I think it is worth struggling for the legacy of Sorel, Bataille, Nietzsche, and other authors whose ideas give room for opposing political interpretations. Sorel's theory of violence is on the side of the oppressed, and therefore cannot really be associated with the far right, which is always on the side of force, or violence of the first type.

Divine violence

Benjamin's essay, "Critique of Violence," was written in the winter of 1920–1, during the tough historical moment of the so-called Red Terror in Russia, after the socialist revolution. According to Benjamin, all our ambitions to decide which violence is legitimate and which is not are trapped within the domain of the law, but the law itself is violence: there is "something rotten in the law."[12] All legal violence is either lawmaking, or law-preserving. It aims either to maintain the existing order of things, or to change it with the new one and establish the new law in place of the old one. Lawmaking and law-preserving violence are two sides of the same coin: both are attached to the power of the state. In both cases, violence is considered the means of achieving certain ends, and when we make our judgments about the ends, we also judge the means as being either justified or unjustified. What Benjamin suggests is that we leave aside the interplay of means and ends, forget the ends, and discuss violence in terms of pure means. This sounds paradoxical, as means are usually thought of as secondary and subordinate to ends. However, as Sami Khatib explains, this emancipation of the mediation from a teleological perspective of the final goal (*Endzweck*) makes good sense.[13] It is an exercise in materialist dialectics indeed. Beyond teleology, within which any act of violence had a purpose, it becomes a pure manifestation. I can break the wall without having any particular goal, just out of pure rage. Well, I cannot make it alone, but *we* can.

In order to explain "pure means," Benjamin refers to Sorel's difference between political and proletarian general strikes. The political strike is an interruption of work that is used by politicians of all sorts, and serves as a means of changing masters or working conditions, while the power structure remains more or less the same, improved and secured. In Benjamin's terms, changing masters or establishing new rules and conditions is a lawmaking violence, whereas the proletarian general strike is anarchistic, or law-destroying. It does not have a positive program or any project for lawmaking. What is the general strike for? This is not the question we should be asking. Just don't think teleologically. It is pure violence – that is, not subordinated to something else outside it. This is the sense of pure means, which Benjamin evokes when he quotes Sorel: "The revolution appears as a revolt, pure and simple, and no place is reserved for sociologists, for fashionable people who are in favor of social reforms, and for Intellectuals who have embraced *the profession of thinking for the proletariat.*"[14]

Since we recognize violence as a pure manifestation, a new distinction emerges – between the mythic and the divine. However, the mythic violence in Benjamin doesn't have a positive link to the immediate will of the people and the workers' strike, as it has in Sorel. Quite the opposite: mythic violence is that which manifests the force of law and therefore the power of the state against which Sorel's proletariat rebelled. Benjamin's example of mythic violence is the Greek myth of Niobe, who was punished for her arrogance: she boasted of having fourteen children, while the goddess Leto only had two; Leto sent her twins, Apollo and Artemis, to kill all of Niobe's children, whose grief turned her into stone. According to Benjamin, Niobe's punishment is an act of lawmaking, where the violence of the law is intimately bound to the power of gods: "Lawmaking is powermaking, assumption on power, and to that extent an immediate manifestation of violence."[15] Another name for this power is fate: something from above that one has to accept. All legal violence, both lawmaking and law-preserving, corresponds to mythic violence, which Benjamin discards as "pernicious," for it manifests the power of the strongest as the force of law. Benjamin uses two terms for all mythic violence – "executive" for lawmaking violence and "administrative" for law-preserving violence: these two functions perfectly coincide in such an "ignominious" institution as the police, which carries out violence in the name of the law.[16]

The second type of violence, which Benjamin calls "divine," contrary to what some people might think, is neither the one that comes from god, nor the one that is committed in the name of god, but rather the one that happens, as it were, in place of god. Imagine a situation, as simple as it is paradigmatic, of someone being brutally beaten by a police officer. For people in countries like Russia, this comes as no surprise: if you see a policeman, hide yourself, for these guys can really turn you into minced meat. This happens, for instance, during protest demonstrations. The law is always on the side of the police officer, whereas nothing seems to be on the side of the people who are beaten. And yet there is something.

I cannot but cite a recent instance. In January 2021, before going out on the protest march against Putin and his group that had retained state power for twenty years, Russians, also non-believers, were saying to each other: "God be with you!" Everybody knew perfectly well that this regime is maintained exclusively by an incredible degree of police violence and fear. Everybody knew that for this action – a simple going out, indeed unauthorized – anybody could have been arrested, beaten up, taken to court on criminal charges, or could lose their jobs, families, and maybe even their lives. Nevertheless, thousands of people in all regions of the huge multinational country, from Vladivostok in the far east to Kaliningrad on the western borders, took the risk and went out, without any hope of changes, just out of rage. "God be with you!" meant that nothing would really help the people on strike, but they were throwing snowballs at the policemen. The situation of state terror clearly demonstrates how the law itself becomes an instance of an absolute and ultimate injustice, which comes as fate. And yet there is still a possibility for another kind of violence, which is outside the law. We do not have the right to resist the representative of the state who wrings our hands, but we still retain this precarious ultimate possibility (suddenly, we have plenty of snow). The only god here is the people's own existence manifested as rage. This is one of the ways to understand the unalloyed, or divine, violence, whose highest manifestation, according to Benjamin, is revolutionary violence.

Divine violence constitutes an opposition to the mythic in all respects:

> If mythic violence is lawmaking, divine violence is law-destroying; if the former sets boundaries, the latter boundlessly destroys them; if mythic violence brings at once guilt and retribution, divine power only expiates; if the former threatens, the latter strikes; if the former is bloody, the latter is lethal without spilling blood.[17]

The example provided by Benjamin himself is extremely problematic. He refers to the punishment of Korah, who was leading a rebellion against Moses and Aaron. According to The Book of Numbers, God destroyed Korah and all of his people together with their families, as well as all those who supported them.[18] This looks like a massacre, but in Benjamin's perspective, it's not. Attention must be paid to the paradoxical definition: "lethal without spilling blood." The ground splits beneath people's feet and the fire from hell swallows them alive. Against all thinkable laws, a terrifying miracle happens as if by itself. As Benjamin explains, in this case "God's judgment strikes privileged Levites, strikes them without warning, without threat, and does not stop short of annihilation. But in annihilating it also expiates, and a profound connection between the lack of bloodshed and the expiatory character of this violence is unmistakable."[19] This is an extreme example, which shows that Benjamin does not idealize or romanticize divine violence. It is not that the "bad" mythic and the "good" divine are in opposition. Divine violence in fact can be anything – from glorious to monstrous – we never know. We are not able to judge whether it was really divine or not, as its expiatory power, according to Benjamin, "is invisible to men." Divine violence is "sovereign" (*waltende*) in two senses. First, it serves no goal. Second, it is outside the law. It has nothing to appeal to; there is no police officer beyond it, no authority, and no God. In Žižek's terms: "There is no big Other guaranteeing its divine nature."[20]

It is precisely because of the absence of any authoritative support – religious, moral, or juridical – that violent deeds outside the law become the full responsibility of those who act: they know that they violate the law. In this regard, Benjamin's reflection on lethal violence is remarkable. Do people have the right to kill each other? No, this right "cannot be conceded."[21] Every such question meets a commandment: "Thou shalt not kill." But this only works within the domain of right. One can follow the commandment or not, but if one decides to break it, one is fully responsible for one's deed: the commandment exists "as a guideline for the actions of persons or communities who have to wrestle with it in solitude and, in exceptional cases, to take on themselves the responsibility of ignoring it."[22] What Benjamin has in mind is a range of cases, from the Judaic tradition, where killing in self-defense is not condemned, to revolutionary terror. The dividing line between the mythic and the divine will be this one: if killing is a means to certain ends within legal order, it is definitely mythic. "I defended the law," says the policemen who killed a person on the street. Against this singular act of mythic violence, an avalanche of people's wrath sets everything on fire. Does this mean that Benjamin justifies terror? One should not jump to such conclusions, because justifying terror would mean making judgments that are already within the domain of the law. He does not justify, does not make judgments about whether something is good or bad, but points to the site whence the violence comes.

Let me provide another example, which, at first glimpse, seems less political. In July 2018, in Moscow, three sisters, Krestina, 19, Angelina, 18, and Maria, 17, killed their father Mikhail Khachaturyan. When they were arrested, they confessed that they had been physically, sexually, and emotionally abused by this man, who kept them in slavery for years. Khachaturyan did not allow the girls to go to school, continuously battering, humiliating, and raping them. He was an authoritative person with lots of power and connections, including in police circles; neighbors and acquaintances were afraid of him. In Russia, domestic violence is not criminalized; there are basically no legal mechanisms to protect women and children in cases like this. And yet, the girls found a way to defend themselves: they attacked the father with a hammer, a knife, and pepper spray while he was sleeping. The girls were charged with premeditated murder, which resulted in jail sentences ranging from eight to twenty years.[23]

This case shows a clear confrontation between the two types of violence according to Benjamin. On the one hand, there is the violence of symbolic order, represented by the figure of the omnipotent father, who, even after his death, continued to terrorize his daughters with the mythic force of the law that defended him in his right as the strongest; that the police and the state legal system were on the side of the father is not surprising. On the other hand, there is a divine violence of the girls, who take full responsibility and admit their guilt for their act of pure and immediate justice that breaks the paternal order of the law. Yes, they kill, they violate the law, but their condemnation and imprisonment are immediately displayed as injustice. It is hard to resist the temptation to interpret this case along the lines of the famous Freudian myth of the murder of the father of the primitive horde by the group of brothers. This collective violent act, according to Freud, marks the beginning of humanity. However, taking a closer look at this analogy through the lens of Benjamin's theory of violence, we can see that the violence of the brothers is mythic in the sense that it is lawmaking: in place of the father's abuse of power, they establish their own law. In contrast, the violence of the sisters is law-destroying, and serves no goal: they rise against fate. Their deed is incommensurate with oedipal power struggles; it opens another dimension of life. No man can judge this.

There seems to be an affinity between Benjamin's divine violence and the idea of divine law, introduced by Hegel in the beginning of the sixth chapter of his *Phenomenology of Spirit*, where he inscribes the analysis of the foundations of traditional gender structure into the dialectics of family and social fields. According to Hegel, divine law is opposed to human law. Human law comprises the domain of public law, or the law of the polis (namely, the Greek *polis*). It represents the world of social articulation and the ethical power of the state, which Hegel compares with the light of the day, and identifies as male. Divine law is an instance of immediate ethical consciousness, which does not need to consult a written law in order to know how to act: it always already knows what to do. It is unconscious and feminine, coming from the realm of the under-world, as Hegel calls it, and prevailing in the family as opposed to the public domain of the state and government. Hegel speaks of Antigone, who dares to bury her brother Polinices in spite of the prohibition imposed by Creon, the king of the city of Thebes. Antigone deliberately violates the human order for the sake of divine law. As Hegel comments on this: "Ethical consciousness is more complete and its guilt purer if it both *knows* the law *beforehand* and the power against which it takes an opposing stance, and it takes them to be violence and wrong, to be an ethical contingency, and then, like Antigone, knowingly commits the crime."[24]

Indeed, the principal difference between Hegel's divine law and Benjamin's divine violence is that the latter is not the law at all. Hegel's Antigone has something substantial above her. The substance, which Hegel calls "pathos," is actualized in the deed of the character. Antigone's pathos is the tradition to which she belongs: as a loving sister, she must bury her brother. In contrast, the Khachaturyan sisters – Krestina, Angelina, and Maria – do not have any pathos. There is nothing above or behind their violent act, which can therefore be understood as pure means. What makes me put these two examples together,

43

besides the attribution of the divine character to certain direct actions, is sisterhood. According to Hegel, "The feminine, as the sister ... has the highest *intimation* of ethical essence."[25] From this stance, we can arrive at the idea of the sovereignty of sisterhood. Unlike brotherhood, always linked to some positive laws and values, it cannot coincide with the site of power manifesting either mythic or human laws, but stands in opposition to it.

In the colonies

Whereas Benjamin's essay evokes an ability to read between the lines and allows diverse interpretations, Frantz Fanon, in *The Wretched of the Earth* (1961), openly and straightforwardly encourages his comrades to rise up in arms. As opposed to the violence of the ruling classes in European countries, which shields itself with "the educational system, whether lay or clerical, the structure of moral reflexes handed down from father to son, the exemplary honesty of workers who are given a medal after fifty years of good and loyal service" and other "aesthetic expressions of respect for the established order,"[26] the violence in the colonies is transparent: "The policeman and the soldier, by their immediate presence and their frequent and direct action, maintain contact with the native and advise him by means of rifle butts and napalm not to budge."[27] The natives are humiliated and deprived of personal freedom; their world is narrow, full of prohibitions, and "can only be called in question by absolute violence."[28] Colonizers want native people to be disciplined and to obey their rules. Such a situation has a negative impact on natives' psychic lives: there is an internal aggression that grows and, without finding a way out, transforms into mental disorders. This is one of the most important implications of the social predicament of mental illness, which Fanon draws from his vast experience of working as a psychiatrist with colonial people.[29]

Neither myths nor rituals are among Fanon's favorites, since they eventually play into the hands of the colonial regime: collective dances and exorcism channel the aggression that has been accumulated in the community and facilitate its peaceful de-escalation. Interestingly, Fanon compares such rituals with volcano eruptions within the limited circle:

At certain times on certain days, men and women come together at a given place, and there, under the solemn eye of the tribe, fling themselves into a seemingly unorganized pantomime, which is in reality extremely systematic, in which ... may be deciphered as in an open book the huge effort of a community to exorcise itself, to liberate itself, to explain itself. There are no limits – inside the circle ... There are no limits – for in reality your purpose in coming together is to allow the accumulated libido, the hampered aggressivity, to dissolve as in a volcanic eruption. Symbolical killings, fantastic rides, imaginary mass murders – all must be brought out. The evil humors are undammed, and flow away with a din as of molten lava.[30]

Temporary relaxation supports the reproduction of violence by the colonial regime. Time and again, African natives express their negative passions in collective ritual performances before returning to their everyday oppressed and depressed condition. According to Fanon, this is not the right way to deal with negative affections. Instead of being neutralized in rituals of exorcism, they must be radicalized and transformed into weapons in the struggle for liberation. Yes, people are possessed, but what possesses them is not demons; it is their own feelings – rage, resentment, humility – that has been repressed. These need to be released, and not expulsed. Yes, natives in the colonies demonstrate aggression and a propensity toward violence, but this general symptomatology is a result of their unbearable conditions. The most effective therapy would be nothing more than a desperate fight, which would give proper scope to their aggression: "At the level of individuals, violence is a cleansing force. It frees the native from his inferiority complex and from his despair and inaction; it makes him fearless and restores his self-respect."[31] At another level, it binds people together and gives them a sense of history and collective destiny. The violence of the natives is a response to the violence of the colonizers. It is brutal, but it has a positive quality: the negation of negation indeed.

A serpent and a spider

Fanon completed and published *The Wretched of the Earth* shortly before his death, in 1961. That same year, Georges Bataille wrote one of his last essays, "Pure happiness." A large part of this essay is dedicated to violence, which Bataille, too, divides into two types. The first type of violence is profane, limited, subordinated to certain practical ends. The second is sacred, unlimited, and sovereign. This division principally corresponds to Bataille's social ontology, which is characterized by the tension between dualism and dialectics: there are always two worlds, or two poles, that are opposite, but they are interconnected and never exist one without another. The profane and the sacred, homogeneous and heterogeneous, discrete and continuous, limited and unlimited – all objects theorized by Bataille – are qualified according to their relevance to one of these poles. There are two types of everything: each thing either circulates within the order of the profane, within its limits, separated from other things and serving certain functions, or is withdrawn from this order into the domain of the sacred, where all borders are erased and death itself appears not as the limit, but as the luxury performance of life. These two poles never converge, but one necessarily produces the other: taboos and limitations of the order of the profane constitute the domain of the sacred, where falls all that is impossible to convert, to make useful, from God to menstrual blood.

In "Pure happiness," unrestrained violence is opposed to the limits vigorously imposed by human reason. What reason does is a constant operation of limitation: thought creates a sphere of things that are thinkable, that is, reducible to the categories of reason. In this operation, something is necessarily excluded, and it is precisely this something that creates the domain of violence, or, as Bataille otherwise calls it, the sacred. Yes, for Bataille, violence and the sacred are often synonymous. This is why those who do not read Bataille carefully enough often ascribe to him the culture of violence. As emphasized by Benjamin Noys: "all too often 'celebrations' of Bataille do just that. However, in breaking the (violently imposed) taboos on violence Bataille is not aiming to increase violence but to examine how these strict taboos generate their own violence."[32]

Bataille's violence is an asymmetrical response to reason's policy of limitations. Reason and violence create a dialectical couple, but this dialectic is not the one of Hegel, who, according to Bataille, "attempts to gain access to the equivalence of thought and violence."[33] It is true that, in his Introduction to the *Phenomenology*, Hegel features violence as the driving force of negativity: "Consciousness suffers this violence at its own hands and brings to ruin its own restricted satisfaction."[34] Such is the movement of the Spirit, violent and desperate, going beyond the limits of itself. However, this movement has a final goal, which "lies at that point where knowledge no longer has the need to go beyond itself, that is, where knowledge works itself out, and where the concept corresponds to the object and the object to the concept."[35] Hegelian violence of thought is a means of achieving the state of absolute knowledge. Therefore, in Bataille's terms, it is itself restricted, or profane: knowledge cannot be absolute, as it will always have "nonknowledge" as its limit. When reason tries to adjust the object to the concept, it does not really assimilate this object, but rather cuts it short. There are leftovers, however, a material excess that it cannot eliminate.

Between reason and violence, there is close reciprocity, whereby reason works as a policeman: what it excludes is the unthinkable, the unspoken, or animality. This is the mechanism of the taboo: nature, as forbidden, constitutes the sacred. However, as Kathryn Yusoff explains, the excluded "returns as a destructive force because it has not been properly accounted for."[36] This can be compared to the process of repression, in a Freudian sense followed by the return of the repressed. The excluded, which is produced by what reason excludes from its domain of useful and comprehensible things, becomes the object of its fundamental interrogation, for which violence "offers itself as the only answer."[37] Bataille further suggests that such an answer "can only come from the outside, from that which thought had to exclude *in order to exist*," and identifies it with god himself: "Is not god an expression of violence offered as a solution?"[38] Here, it is important to understand that god exists not by himself, but precisely as this responsive violence.[39]

It is divine not only in the sense that it is sacred, but also in the sense that it is sovereign. There is nothing above and beyond it, and, in contrast to the violence of the first type (the police of reason), it does not serve anything: "Full *violence* can be the means to no end. It would be subordinate to no goal."[40] In his notes to the essay, Bataille explains: "Violence reduced to a means is an end in the service of a means – it is a god become a servant."[41]

There are obvious parallels and intersections between Bataille's concept of violence and the ones suggested by Sorel, Fanon, and Benjamin. The exclusion of animality, which produces the excess of violence and can be understood in psychoanalytic terms, as repression and the return of the repressed, bears some structural similarity to the suppression of aggression that must find a way out, according to Fanon. Both Fanon and Bataille interpret social processes with an eye to the Freudian theory of the unconscious and see correlation between the lives of individuals and the structures of communities. However, Fanon's focus is *stricto sensu* political, whereas Bataille deploys a speculative account on reason and its relation to its Other. Suggestion that this Other as the site of violence is god, as well as its definition as serving no ends, or the sovereign, highly resonates with both Benjamin's concept of the divine violence and Sorel's general strike. Like Sorel, Bataille derives pure – that is, unsubordinated – violence from myth and opposes it to the pragmatics of reason. Like Benjamin, he calls it divine. Bataille's violence is a general strike, too, but in a different sense – the one implemented by the theory of the general economy, to which I will return a bit later. His violence is god, but not the God of theology: it is "the animal god," whose "incomparable purity" and "violence above laws" Bataille invites us to discover.[42]

With respect to all parallels drawn between the theories that inscribe the apology of emancipatory violence in the dialectics of the double negation, the originality of Bataille's project calls for a closer examination. Here is the distinction that he introduces in "Pure happiness":

I imagine two kinds of Violence.
The victim of the first kind is led astray.
It is the Violence of a rapid train at the moment of the death of the despairing person who willfully threw himself on the tracks.
The second kind is that of the serpent or the spider, that of an element which is irreconcilable to the order wherein the possibility of being is given, which turns you to stone. It does not confound but slips; it dispossesses, it paralyzes, it fascinates before you might oppose anything to it.
This kind of Violence, the second kind, is in itself imaginary. It is nevertheless the faithful image of a violence, this measureless violence without

form, without method – that at any moment I can equate with God.[43]

In the image of the train that will run us down, a reader can discern the idea of the limited and limiting violence. A policeman with a truncheon can play the role of the train, and what Bataille calls "reason" can play the role of the policeman. However, the second kind of violence, according to Bataille, introduces something new: the violence of the nonhuman. It is nonanthropomorphic and nonanthropocentric. What is the violence of a serpent or a spider? Even if they do not really harm, the sudden appearance of these or other animals can give us a scare that we won't be able to control. Serpents and spiders embody an imaginary violence that, in Bataille's view, equates to god. Note that serpents and spiders are sacred or scary not as such, but only in our imagination, in that they are produced not by the sleep of reason, but by its obsessive wakefulness and desire to control everything. By themselves, serpents and spiders are indifferent. They do not intend to do violence. A serpent can, of course, attack people and other animals, but the scare that it gives us does not come from our estimation of the real danger that it constitutes. Replace a serpent or a spider with any other animal whose appearance immediately terrifies you, before you apply reasoning – and this will be your personal god of violence. I have mine, too. I don't mind spiders, but I am so scared by some other species that I cannot even name them.

The uncontrollable affection provoked by non-human violence is not necessarily terror or fear. The divine violence of the nonhuman that affects us can really be anything. A serpent, a spider, a new bacterium or virus, a hurricane, permafrost melting in Siberia, radioactivity, forest fires, methane blow-outs: all these present us with an image that differs from our conventional understanding of violence as a negative agency of certain individuals or groups of human beings, including anthropomorphic gods.

Nonhuman violence is without a subject: no one really commits it, no one is to blame. The god of violence belongs to the world of immediacy and immanence, which, in his book *Theory of Religion* (1948), Bataille calls animality.[44] As Benjamin Noys comments: "The world of animals is a world without difference because animals know nothing of negativity, and thereby know nothing of difference."[45] Bataille's animality is a utopian realm, a conceptual fantasy of an indifferent continuity inaccessible by human beings. Animals eat one another, and those that eat do not really differentiate themselves from those they eat, do not conceive them as separate objects. I cannot blame a wolf for eating a calf. Predation and other forms of violence inherent in the animal world are compared to the movement of the sea waves swallowing each other: "Every animal is in the world like water in water."[46] If there are differences, they are quantitative and not qualitative; therefore, we cannot really speak about inequalities among animals, or about power relations: "The lion is not the king of the beasts: in the movement of the waters he is only a higher wave overturning the other, weaker ones."[47]

Although elsewhere he defines animals as "essentially free beings,"[48] in *Theory of Religion* Bataille admits that their indifference and alienness to juridical and moral laws does not mean absolute freedom. All living organisms, including humans, depend on their environments at least to the extent that they need to eat. Natural needs limit their autonomy. Humans are animals that want to break these limitations, which they associate with animality, but in their desire to be independent of nature they jump into a bigger enslavement as they create the world of taboo, usefulness, reason, language, and labor, to which other animals remain alien. This new, human world, in Bataille's words, is profane, whereas excluded animality becomes sacred, becomes god (note that the most ancient gods were animals). This is how the disparity between human and nonhuman violence reflects the paradox of freedom. Striving for the autonomy from the laws of nature, human beings depart from animality and surround themselves with new laws and prohibitions, thus producing the phantasmatic divinity of the nonhuman.

I can imagine the general strike of the proletariat, a revolution, a popular uprising, or liberation struggles of people under colonial rule. I can stand alongside those who are engaged in these fights, according to my sense of justice, as well as ethical and political attitudes. But I cannot take the side of a serpent or a spider in a similar way. How can I identify with the site of nonhuman violence if it is the site of alterity, on the exclusion of which any identity is based? This seems to be an impossible task, and all the more challenging. Bataille's enterprise is, I think, very much about this: finding an inhuman element within the human, which will connect me to the serpent, to the volcano, or to the sun. This is what I mean when I say that there is something deeply Socratic in Bataille, but one can also say that there is something deeply Bataillean in Socrates, who points out the resemblance of the sun to the human eye.

2

General Economy

Two kinds of violence presented in "Pure happiness" correspond to the two kinds of economy that Bataille analyzes in the first volume of his fundamental book *The Accursed Share* (1949). The volume begins with the admission that, for some years, the author was embarrassed to have to say that he was working on "a book of political economy."[1] It was a very ambitious project, indeed, mainly because the sort of political economy proposed by Bataille seems to have nothing to do with traditional works in the field. It starts from the critique of political economy as we know it. This is quite a Marxian gesture: remember that Marx criticizes bourgeois economists for considering a worker not as a human being, but as a working horse, and labor not as a human essence, but as a commodity that can be sold or bought, and then applies a class perspective to the analysis of the system of capitalist production based on the exploitation of human and natural resources. Bataille's criticism is different: in his view, the main problem of economists is that they discuss production rather than consumption and only focus on human affairs, without taking into consideration "the general problem of nature."[2] The vast majority of economic science takes its objects as isolated phenomena – for instance, the car industry or the agricultural sector – but the principal question remains: "Shouldn't productive activity as a whole be considered in terms of the modifications it receives from its surroundings or brings about in its surroundings? In other words, isn't there a need to study the system of human production and consumption within a much larger framework?"[3]

By "a much larger framework," Bataille means "the general problems that are linked to the movement of energy on the globe."[4] He was inspired by the idea of founding such a syncretic science that would consider the physical, geological, sexual, philosophical, and political processes in their mutual intersection. He did not have enough discipline to collate this science into a proper system, but he gave it a good name – general economy. This is an extraordinary precursor of the new domain of energy humanities, wherein global warming and other major contemporary ecological issues are addressed beyond the framework of positivist natural sciences.[5] For the general economy, energy is not only what matters, but what matters the most. Its currents define all economic life. Today, when our existence depends on oil prices rather than on God's providence, or something of this kind, we are very aware of this. We are, however, used to thinking of energy as a limited resource for all productive activities. For Bataille, this was not the case. He saw the problem not in the lack but in the excess of energy, the ultimate source of which is the sun.

We, living organisms, receive more energy than we really need and can accommodate. In this sense, we are not poor, but rich, as is everything and everybody on Earth. It is because of this excessive energy that all animals and plants can grow and reproduce, but even growth and reproduction cannot exhaust what we receive for no cost. What limits the overall growth is "the size of the terrestrial space,"[6] within which animals and plants develop, invade the land, assemble and replace each other. Living forms rotate incessantly. Life itself is an extravagant luxury, with death as its culminating point.

The general economy is the name not only for the science, invented by Bataille, but also for the complex phenomena that it describes. It is opposed to the restricted economy, or economics in the conventional sense, which comprises various human activities within the closed circle of means and ends. The general economy is not human-sized, but planetary, or cosmic. Its basic principle is expenditure, as opposed to the goals of accumulation and growth that are characteristic of restricted human economies, such as the capitalist economy.

On a global scale, as Bataille says, there is no growth, "but only a luxurious squandering of energy in every form."[7] Restricted economies attempt to appropriate its flows and subordinate them to particular finite ends, from mere physical survival to the creation of new markets, but, after all, "beyond our immediate ends, man's activity in fact pursues the useless and infinite fulfillment of the universe."[8] There is always a limit of growth, and an excess that must be spent this or that way. This excess is called "the accursed share." The more we produce, the more we need to waste. If every surplus is invested in further growth of the system, like capital, a catastrophic outcome is just a matter of time. Warfare is an example of such an outcome: the prospect of nuclear war, in particular, was a matter of concern for Bataille and his contemporaries.

Be like the sun!

A superabundance of energy comes from the sun: "solar energy is the source of life's exuberant development. The origin and essence of our wealth are given in the radiation of the sun, which dispenses energy – wealth – without any return. The sun gives without ever receiving."[9] *Be like the sun!* – this is basically Bataille's motto for the possible future of the political economy adjusted to the planetary scale and balanced with the ecological whole. If we want our economies to be commensurate with our environments, we have to become solar. Bataille's general economy is paradoxically rational: what it suggests is that we recognize the limits of growth and think through strategies of nonproductive expenditure as self-conscious activity. We should stop being greedy and stop striving for individual growth, which results in planetary energy restoring its balance in an uncontrolled and catastrophic way. Nonproductive expenditure must be taken seriously and organized as an economy of gifts without reciprocation – a glorious economy.

In *The Accursed Share*, Bataille tackles historical practices and traditions that represent different approaches to the problem of excess and the ways of dealing with it: sacrifices made by the Aztecs, potlach rituals, Islam, Lamaism, capitalism and bourgeois society, the Soviet system and the American initiative of the Marshall plan. Are there examples of the general economy in the sense that he implements when he connects it to the laws of the universe? Not really. There is always something wrong with the ways in which we interpret gifts. One would expect the last case analyzed by Bataille in his book – the Marshall plan – to be painted as a perspective solution, as it relates to the distribution of excessive American wealth among European countries devastated by World War Two. However, as Bataille emphasizes, even this is a Western political project, created in opposition to the Soviet Union, and considered by its proponents as an investment in the future of capitalism.

The general economy as self-conscious activity is something different, for what Bataille means by self-consciousness basically equates to sovereignty. It cannot be an investment, but only pure expenditure. Self-consciousness, in his interpretation, "has nothing as its object,"[10] meaning that it does not want to increase its resources, does not strive to grow and prosper. Self-consciousness goes beyond the limits of the individual; its point of view is not that of the living organism seeking out where to get more stuff, but that of the planetary whole. The transition from consciousness of the individual, determined by needs and interests, to the generous self-consciousness is finally identified by Bataille as the last act of the transition "from animal to man."[11]

This claim, which he immediately tries to detach from teleology (from the idea of the final goal of historical humanity, the achievement of which, according to Alexander Kojeve, would coincide with the end of history), today sounds obscenely anthropocentric, but let us take a closer look at it. Bataille's generalization of all living organisms that behave in accordance with either their natural needs or their private interests as animals echoes Hegel's description of economic estrangement and the division of labor given in the chapter of his *Phenomenology of Spirit* beautifully titled "The Spiritual Kingdom of Animals and Deception; or the Crux of the Matter (*die Sache selbst*),"[12] where Hegel explains that individuals, indeed, do think that they are pursuing their private interests – for instance, when they sell commodities that they produce and try to cheat on each other – but this is only an illusion. In fact, without realizing it, these people contribute to the development of the overall economic structure. Bataille's point, however, is different: yes, individuals pursue their interests, just like other animals that search for food when they are hungry, and entire national economic systems, too, can be compared to such egotistic individuals, but even if they think that they are struggling for universal prosperity, they actually contribute to overall planetary destruction.

This thesis finds endorsement in today's ecological issues: technogenic catastrophes, air and water pollution, or the difficult problem of waste are nothing more than the effects of dizzying economic growth rates. In this sense, the transition from individual to human will be the change of perspective, taking the side of the general, solar, or cosmic, that is, paradoxically, of the nonhuman. The question rises though: where should we get the resources for such generosity? Bataille's response would be that we are always already inherently solar. As planetary beings, we have our moments of "glory" – from something as kind and innocent as sharing, caring, and giving gifts, through arts, play, and self-abandonment of eroticism, to the most violent destructive acts of sacrifice or extermination. We rationalize these lavish acts (for instance, we make sacrifices in order to gain the favor of gods, or exterminate certain animal species for epidemiological reasons, for the sake of a healthier humanity), and thus try to inscribe them within the logic of restricted economies, but in fact we unconsciously follow general cosmic laws of excessively squandering energy and wealth.

Wombats and ethics

I do think, however, that Bataille's account in *The Accursed Share* of animals as restricted individuals is not fully thought through: there are reasons for believing that the inherent solarity that he relates to self-consciousness is indeed animal, if we treat animals not as individuals but first and foremost as collective beings. From my perspective, animality is a way of existence beyond the individual; it is a form of primordial togetherness that can provide us with alternative models of the common. We are still not able to estimate the extent to which animals dance, sing, play; to give proper respect to their plasticity, enthusiasm, or wisdom.

Think of the wombats that, during the devastating Australian bushfire season in 2019–20, saved the lives of many other smaller animals by sheltering them in their large and complex burrows. There was a hell on Earth: more than a billion living creatures were wiped out by fire, but not the ones that managed to hide underneath the ground. When news about the incredible kindness of wombats rescuing other animals begun to circulate, scientists hurriedly came up with explanations that the wombats didn't do so intentionally, but only by chance: these large mammals usually dig multiple spacious burrows, and while they are sleeping in just one of them, others may incidentally become hide-outs for the surrounding wildlife.[13] Why was it so important, for natural scientists, to articulate the idea that the Australian wombats did not really exhibit altruism, solidarity, and care for neighboring species, but only instinctual behavior? Because solidarity and altruism fall within the domain of morality to which, according to our scientific policy, animals remain alien.

What if, however, opening their burrows up to other residents of the burning bush, wombats are expressing something that cannot be understood within the framework of Darwinian biology, which sees animals as primitive egoistic individuals struggling for survival? What if altruism and solidarity are precisely those forms of behavior that we cheaply label as instinctual? What if animals do not really need morals and other forms of mediation, because their relation to their territories is different from the private property with which human beings are so obsessed? As famous Russian anarchist Piotr Kropotkin demonstrated in his book *Mutual Aid: A Factor of Evolution* (1902), the struggle for survival is not the only one, and not even the main force of the development of life on Earth: various species survive because they cooperate, communicate, and help each other.[14] Today's ecological thinking discovers this new possible way of addressing nature. Thus, Timothy Morton's call for solidarity with "nonhuman people" presumes that solidarity is not something specifically human, but "the default affective environment of the top layers of the Earth's crust."[15] In Imre Szeman's framing, solarity is "a form of solidarity that always already attends to the non-human and the Earth, to the lightness of limits and the depth of responsibility that comes when we tarry with the infinite."[16]

Coming back to Bataille's perspective, I suggest that the wombat-like generosity can be regarded as a kind of underdeveloped part of human animality, a properly solar, or cosmic, part repressed by our restricted economies that constitute us as Darwinian individuals greedy for resources, struggling for survival, and tending to grow. This greed is not so much real animal hunger, as it is projected onto animals that could equally be described in opposite terms, in the language of the general, or solar economy. Wombats do not need an ethical turn to share their living facilities with mice and lizards. Applying Bataille's theory of animality as immanence, I suggest that, for the wombat, the act of sharing is not "good," but rather indifferent, not unlike a wolf eating a calf. I am not sure though whether "indifferent" is the right word. I would say that an animal can be equally enthusiastic in a violent act of killing as in generosity of caring. What human animals do is make ethical judgments about which acts are good, and which are evil. In order to be like wombats, we need a complex mediation of self-consciousness that implies a radical ethical turn: "Changing from the perspectives of *restrictive* economy to those *of general* economy actually accomplishes a Copernican transformation: a reversal of thinking – and of ethics."[17]

Elevated into a self-conscious human strategy, which takes the indifferent generosity of the sun as its model and transforms it into a new ethics with regard to the ecological whole, this economy becomes the economy of gift as opposed to one of exchange. It privileges consumption over production and expenditure over accumulation. Allan Stoekl, who explores Bataille's theory for the twenty-first century, addresses the general economy as an ethical turn in the following way:

Not nuclear war, but the channeling of excess in ways that ensure survival so that more excess can be thrown off. And (one can continue along these lines) not generalized ecocide, but an affirmation of another energy, another religion, another waste, entailing not so much a steady state sustainability (with what stable referent? Man?) but instead a postsustainable state in which we labor in order to expend, not conserve.[18]

Importantly in this regard, Stoekl makes a distinction between destructive waste and nonproductive expenditure. Contemporary restrictive economies, based on the processes of burning fossil fuels, are in fact economies of waste, that have to be confronted by the general economy: it is time to learn to expend consciously instead of wasting blindly.

How to imagine such a nonrestrictive society? Bataille provides an example of extreme poverty in India contrasted to excessive wealth in the US: "General economy suggests, therefore, as a correct operation, a transfer of American wealth to India without reciprocation."[19] This sounds like a simple, but impossible, solution. Why? Because we are used to thinking about such matters in terms of restricted human economies. We consider social life as consisting of interactions between separate objects, individuals or groups, national states and other units that share their specific needs, interests, or functions; whereas the general economy only comprises the planetary whole and its equilibriums. The capitalist economy, which can only treat nature as a resource, is incompatible with the politics of generosity. Therefore, the reversal of ethics alone is not enough. According to Szeman, Bataille's Copernican transformation of thinking and ethics from the restricted to the general "necessitates a politics of revolution rather than reform."[20] Bataille himself doesn't really bring forward any explicit program or strategy for political change. His attitude is the one of an eccentric researcher, who does not have a project but suggests his radical hypothesis about the structure of the universe. I find this hypothesis decent enough to be introduced within our recent context.

Pandemic squander

Starting in winter 2019–20, COVID-19 quickly developed into a full-on global pandemic that has already caused nearly five million deaths worldwide and has led to a serious economic, political, and – first and foremost – existential crisis. Throughout 2020, governments of different national states proposed different responses, the most obvious of which were quarantines and lockdowns. The deadly infection revealed the fact that humanity is vulnerable and that neither the global capitalist system nor nation-states can guarantee the security of the people, in spite of all the restrictions introduced at local levels that went as far as violating basic human rights and freedoms, such as the freedom of movement. One by one, national states started to close their borders. Yet what did not stop moving freely was the virus; on the level of practical materiality, it demonstrated how everything is connected on multiple levels – people and other animals, weather conditions, surfaces of objects, interfaces and infrastructures, currency rates, science, emotions, air pollution, cultural developments, and industry machines.

Governments knew only the language of restrictive economies, with which they were trying to talk to the virus: no, you cannot enter, my country is closed! Some of them, however, were forced to understand the necessity to share, and began to adjust minor elements of the general economy, like giving compensation to those who lost their jobs. The pandemic showed that one cannot even save a restrictive economy from the destructive excess of the nonhuman without introducing such elements. But it also showed that the question is not how to save the restricted economy – that is, how to save really existing capitalism – but how to replace it with something more general and more generous, with something glorious, as Bataille would say.

If we were to think of human responses to this planetary challenge on the general scale, perhaps we would have to listen to today's communist thinkers, such as Slavoj Žižek, who discusses the possibilities of "global coordination and collaboration,"[21] or Panagiotis Sotiris, who suggests using state power "to channel resources from the private sector to socially necessary directions."[22] Are there still reasons for believing that the human race is capable of reshaping the entire system of the world economy according to the principles of solidarity, gratuitousness, sharing, and thinking of the whole? The answer is "yes," since the overall reaction to the pandemic cannot be reduced to restrictive measures. In fact, the crisis gave rise to new social and individual initiatives that developed some perspective elements of the general economy, from more traditional gestures of solidarity – financial aid to the most affected countries or groups, sending them medical equipment for free, volunteering, and so on – to providing free access to electronic museums, libraries, and other cultural and educational products. Such elements of self-consciousness often come from people at the local level and thus actualize what is called civil society, as opposed to the states with their security policies.

Restricted local economies hastened to isolate particular units. Countries closed their borders first, then provinces and cities; then families locked themselves inside their apartments, and individuals started to develop habits of social distance and to defend their bodies with face masks, glasses, gloves, and sanitizers. Indeed, these measures seemed reasonable given that they were taken in order to curb the outbreak, thus preventing healthcare systems from becoming overloaded and gaining time until effective vaccines were developed. However, in a situation of global inequality, throwing all countries upon their own resources led to Darwinian strategies of the survival of the fittest, which, for instance, in some areas – due to the lack of medical infrastructure like beds and ventilators for intensive treatment – compelled doctors to make choices about whose lives are worth struggling for (as in the cases when infected elderly people were left without medical care). Furthermore, development of the vaccine market in the direction of capitalist concurrence introduced a new level of political disintegration (one cannot travel to Europe with the Russian vaccine, for example).

When we apply Bataille's theory of the general economy to the pandemic, climate change, environmental crisis, and other contemporary global challenges, they appear as signs of the squandering of nature being reinforced by anthropogenic factors – industry, agriculture, tourism, extraction of fuels, and so on – that at the end of the day becomes fatal for humans. People infected with COVID-19 who cannot receive medical treatment because hospitals are overwhelmed; whales and seabirds that die after eating plastic items; burning forests in Australia, the US, Greece, the Russian Far East, and Siberia; reindeer-breeders and their herds exposed to the anthrax outbreak that was caused by the melting of permafrost on Yamal Peninsula; the disappearance of wild bees and other creatures as a result of the global processes that humanity has provoked by its economic activities, and now cannot control – all seem to become offerings to the planetary debauchery irradiated by the sun. Human beings with their restrictive economies are the active part of this. We think that we are struggling for survival or working for prosperity, but altogether our economic agencies only contribute to the planetary feast that is indistinguishable from a plague.

3

Restrictive Violence of Capital

The destructive aspect of the solar economy, out-
lined by Bataille, relates to the violence of the
nonhuman. I suppose that the two kinds of economy and the two kinds of violence correlate in
the following way: human violence – the one of
the train with us lying on the track – belongs to the
domain of the restricted economy that comprises
all sorts of practical activities of human beings
within the circle of means and goals, whereas nonhuman violence, or violence of the second kind,
refers to the excess of energy at planetary level,
and therefore can be also called "solar." In view
of contemporary theoretical debates on the clash
between humans and nature, let me put it like
this: what Bataille meant by restricted economy

was not only capitalism or Soviet communism, which he criticized for its cult of production, but something more fundamental, deriving from the antagonistic relation between nature and humanity, when the latter pretends to be separate from the former and to manipulate it.

Let me expand this theory further and suggest that what today we call the "Anthropocene," too, can be accounted for in terms of a restricted economy. The profane violence of the Anthropocene resonates with the restricted violence of reason, which excludes what it cannot convert into its object (the nonhuman) and thus produces an excess that returns as repressed, rebels as oppressed, or, in Bataille's terms, rises as the God of violence. The same can be said, more closely, about the Capitalocene, which Jason W. Moore defines as "the historical era shaped by the endless accumulation of capital."[1] Finding economic reasons and excuses for the unprecedented violence toward living beings of all kinds, capitalism becomes a driving force of massive extinction.

The term "Capitalocene" brings more concretism, as it perfectly reflects the direct correspondence between the modern restricted economy and the violence of the first type, with all elements already presented with regard to human violence extended to nature. At a certain level it is comparable to the force, or the violence, of the state, in Sorel's definition, if we treat nature as the exploited. It is mythic, if we refer to Benjamin's conception, for it establishes and preserves the restrictive force of the laws of economic growth and accumulation. It is indeed colonial, wherein what is being colonized is not only the people, but the inhabited territories treated by the colonizers as resources free of cost and available for the production of profit.

Another term for this kind of violence is "banal." The term comes from Hanna Arendt's concept of the "banality of evil" as violence done by those who refuse to think and who blindly obey the laws. Expanding this concept up to our politics toward other species, Kathryn Yussoff speaks of the banal violence that is "located in practices, from the targeted violence of habitat destruction to the banal violence of configuring spaces exclusively around human proclivities (or the proclivities of capital), . . . from palm oil in shampoo to the effect of 'Roundup' on amphibians."[2] Another Yusoff definition for human violence refers to Judith Butler's differentiation between lives that matter – or grievable lives – and lives that do not. Again, applying it to the human–nonhuman worlds, Yusoff describes it as "normative": we exterminate entire species without conceiving this as violence, because we are not sensitive to their lives and deaths.[3]

What if pandemics, climate change, and other phenomena that we consider to be the thread for the existence of humanity are manifestations of the violence of the second type, or the divine violence of the nonhuman, which "offers itself as the only answer" to the banal, normative, restrictive violence of capital? Saying "anthropogenic climate change" seizes two in one: the first kind of violence (anthropogenic), and the nonhuman, literally solar, response to it (climate change). Summer 2021: heatwaves kill about 500 people in Canada, melts cars in Kuwait, leads to deadly floods in Germany, the Netherlands, Belgium, and the south of Russia; forest fires light up the sky in Yakutia and Greece. In neighboring areas, solar violence smells like smog.

Today's ecological sentience poses an impressive image of the human race abusing nature, on the one hand, and, on the other, nature as either a passive victim or a vengeful force sending floods, fires, tsunamis, grasshoppers, and new stronger viruses that mutate in direct proportion to our advancing technologies of immunization against them. As Slavoj Žižek puts it: "When nature is attacking us with viruses, it is in a way sending our own message back to us. The message is: what you did to me, I am now doing to you."[4] It is true, indeed, especially if we think about the ecological factors that resulted in a mutation of the coronavirus to the extent that it became so contagious and dangerous for human beings: namely, about the slaughter of wild animals, industrial farming, and urban development that destroyed animals' natural habitat, and about the economical processes behind all of this.[5]

The indifference of nature

Apparently, nonhuman violence can be understood as a reaction to human violence, and things like climate change or the pandemic can be interpreted as violent acts analogous to proletarian strikes, revolutionary movements, and decolonizing struggles, as if Mother Earth could manifest its unwillingness to be exploited or colonized, and its capacity to fight back.[6] Such a perspective endows nature with serious political vigor, given that both the virus and global warming, with their long chain of consequences, put in jeopardy the entire global system of restricted economies, or, to be blunt, global capitalism.

However, holding on to the Bataillean approach, I would like to note that this jeopardy only exists in humans' restrictive worldview: on the planetary scale, the destruction of a certain economy – say, Russian, Chinese, or even American – is just another luxurious gesture. Addressing nature in terms of emancipatory politics is replete with translating solar violence into the language of means and ends, that is, of the restricted economy. Nevertheless, we can use this translation, keeping in mind that something essential might get lost in it, and the original "message" seriously differs from the one that we receive. In nature, there is no "me" and "you"; the whole does not behave as an individual, does not act responsively and all the more intentionally. Its turbulences are indifferent to human affairs. Asymmetrical to the restrictive violence of capital or the Anthropocene, the divine violence of the nonhuman can therefore appear more chaotic. One of Bataille's own favored examples is volcano eruption: one cannot do anything about its appearance that shows how fragile are all our constructions. It is important, however, that such violence was not there from the very beginning, but emerges as a response to restricted violence. By this I mean that a volcano was definitely there long before us, but we are the ones who perceive its eruption as violence, and not, say, as fireworks of the Earth.

This ambiguity comes out in the Gaia paradigm, formulated in the 1970s by James Lovelock and Lynn Margulis, and recently developed in the works of such authors as Isabelle Stengers, Bruno Latour, and Donna Haraway. The Earth is almost personified by Lovelock and Margulis, who give it the name of a goddess, who, in Greek mythology, gave birth to everything, and was responsible for further fertility. In their hypothesis, Gaia is a synergetic self-regulating system which always keeps the balance in the interactions between organic and non-organic elements.[7] Of course, they didn't mean to say that Gaia was literally a living organism. Moreover, there are reasons to bring this hypothesis, which can be traced back to Vladimir Vernadsky's theory of the biosphere,[8] into proximity with Bataille's planetary economy, which also balances itself on the level of energy flows. However, in contrast to Bataille's planetary whole, Gaia can easily be portrayed as a living being endowed with a kind of reason and affections, with whom humanity could potentially negotiate, or even sign a contract, as was suggested by Michel Serres.[9] As Latour admits: "In any case, how could we avoid the traps of anthropomorphism, if it is true that we are living from now on in the era of the Anthropocene!"[10]

According to Isabelle Stengers, modern ecological crisis can be understood as the intrusion of Gaia: "Gaia is ticklish and that is why she must be named as a being. We are no longer dealing (only) with a wild and threatening nature, nor with a fragile nature to be protected, nor a nature to be mercilessly exploited. The case is new." Endowing Gaia with sensitivity, Stengers sees in her intrusion a kind of willful act, but importantly remarks that this act is not an invitation for any sort of dialog:

> Gaia, she who intrudes, asks nothing of us, not even a response to the question she imposes. Offended, Gaia is indifferent to the question "who is responsible?" and doesn't act as a righter of wrongs – it

seems clear that the regions of the Earth that will be affected first will be the poorest on the planet, to say nothing of all those living beings that have nothing to do with the affair.[11]

This conception is ambivalent: on the one hand, Gaia is ticklish and offended; on the other, Gaia is indifferent, for, unlike us humans, she is not threatened by capitalist destruction of the environment – her existence as a living planet will continue with the participation of other beings, such us microorganisms, that will survive our apocalypse. This second aspect of indifference brings the intrusion of Gaia closer to what I address here, with a reference to Bataille, as the violence of the nonhuman. This reference is a good antidote to the "traps of anthropomorphism" of the Gaia hypothesis, even if we retain its important implications concerning gender distribution: a restrictive economy (Anthropocene, capital) that violates the Earth is male.

The indifference of nature and the incommensurability of the two languages, two economies, and two kinds of violence – to put it bluntly, the human and the planetary – do not mean, however, that general politics, relevant to the general economy, is not possible. As I already emphasized humanity can and must, according to Bataille, think of the economic models that will overcome the restrictedness of existing forms of exchange and production, which always end up with destruction, be it warfare, climate change, pandemic, or the like. A general economy as a project for humanity would take the luxurious character of nature as its starting point and develop it into elevated forms of self-consciousness that will transfer planetary destruction or waste into nonproductive expenditures, of a proper gift economy. Behaving restrictedly, that is, competing, striving for profit, accumulation, and growth, is not self-conscious. It is a mere survival strategy of individual organisms, be they humans or other animals, but also entire nation-states that, particularly in the face of crisis, act as egotistic individuals. Becoming self-conscious means, economy-wise, learning to share.

A plea for altruism that takes nonhuman nature as its model is adopted by contemporary philosophers such as Luce Irigaray, who claims that the future, if there is to be one at all, will be one of sharing: "starting from the sharing of organic and inorganic nature, it would be possible to elaborate a way of thinking and living that is ecological, instead of economic – in other words, non-possessive, non-appropriative, but participatory with regard to a greater whole."[12] In Irigaray's view, learning to share is an urgency in our economies because "the prospects for life on Earth depend on it."[13] The ecology that, in this statement, is mobilized to replace economy, seems to resonate with Bataille's general economy that must replace the restricted one. However, it doesn't seem to account for the violent aspects of a "greater whole." The urgency of today's ecology – to save life on Earth – seems to send it back to the all-too-human register of means and goals, whereas Bataille's sun shines aimlessly, and all life on Earth is nothing but an effect of its sovereign violence. We must learn to share not because we want to live, but because generosity breaks with the restrictive logic of survival.

Phoenix

For all that, I dare assume that there is something wrong with the ethics of sharing. When I try to think about it, I feel a kind of nausea: honestly, does not "learning to share" in these days have a false ring to it, and leave a saccharine stickiness of hypocrisy? Isn't there too much sharing in the air? We work in co-working spaces and live in co-living spaces; we donate and support; we are happy to share experiences and expenses, within reasonable limits. It is nice to be generous, and we all try to be so as much as we can. However, within a restricted capitalist economy, based on accumulation and ownership, where things are not supposed to be distributed for free, but possessed and exchanged at a profit, our regular practices of sharing are nothing more than occasional elements that slightly balance this system. These practices are a parody of gifts just as team-building in the office is a parody of collectivity. If we push our generosity to the limit, we will find ourselves in an awkward position of a loner conveying all their property and money to impostors. The one who shares absolutely is failed; at the end of the day, everything that, like the sun, gives itself without reckoning, seems to be devastated, exhausted, eaten up. As Amanda Boetzkes comments on the place of solar energy in Bataille's ecological thinking, "a global *infrastructure* that drew from a freely available source is inimical to capitalism's restricted energy economy."[14]

And yet, nonrepayable gifts are a necessary condition of the possibility of existence of human restrictive economies. In order to produce commodities, we need natural resources; we cut wood, we mine coal and iron, we pump oil, we generate power from wind and water, we gather fruits and vegetables, we consume animals and use their labor. At the beginning there is always a gift of nature or something or someone that, for the one who is taking, counts as nature. It is just that, as far as nature or what counts as nature is not recognized as a giver, its gifts are not recognized as gifts, but taken as immediately available gratuitous goods. For modern capitalist states and corporations, crude oil, natural gas, wood, or water are not really "given," but are simply present and usable. Capital develops from so-called primitive accumulation and colonization, from taking lands, together with their resident populations, enslaving them, and exploiting all human and nonhuman resources – workforce, fuels, minerals, animals, plants, etc. – for the production of profit.

The initial moment of appropriation of something that is given can be categorized, in terms of Michel Serres, as a parasitic act. The parasite lives at the expense of the other, who is called the host; it attaches itself to the body of the host or digs inside it and eats it. A parasitic relation is not mutual, since a parasite does not give anything back to the host, who provides him with both home and nourishment, although one parasite can itself become a host to another. According to Serres, the entire system of the world economy arranges itself into one-sided parasitic chains, wherein all use and exchange values are preceded by "the abuse value."[15] The ultimate and universal host is nature, on whose body we dwell. It is not parasitic on anything, does not take anything, but can only give.

But then comes an interesting dilemma: how is it possible that the host keeps giving instead of simply dying of exhaustion, which would entail the death of the parasite given the lack of subsistence? This dilemma is reflected in today's ecological alarmism: we take too much from the planet, give nothing in return, and thus slowly but surely destroy our own natural habitat. And yet there is a parasitic belief that, somehow, what nature gives to us will, miraculously, never end, and even if the host's resources are limited, they won't be entirely depleted – or, better, they are drawn again and again from the very depletion and exhaustion of the host. Serres calls this the "daily miracle of the parasite" and evokes the image of the phoenix, a bird that burns up and then reappears out of its own ashes: "It is always the *table d'hôte* and the phoenix of the hosts. Parasitism doesn't stop. The host repeatedly is reborn from his ashes."[16]

This image cannot but evoke the closing paragraphs of Hegel's *Philosophy of Nature*, where the aim of nature is presented as death of its own accord or self-annihilation for the sake of the spirit: "The purpose of nature is to extinguish itself, and to break through its rind of immediate and sensuous being, to consume itself like a phoenix in order to emerge from this externality rejuvenated as spirit."[17] What the phoenix offers is not a normal gift, but a sacrifice. It sacrifices itself or, as Hegel puts it, consumes itself, but always awakens anew. The phoenix of nature is alight like a living sun: a burning bird.

A special role in this mythic structure is accorded to fire as the elemental medium of the sacrifice. As Michael Marder argues in *Pyropolitics*, in traditional sacrificial rites, spiritual content that belongs to gods is supposed to be extracted from material forms by being held over flames. In other words, fire transforms matter into spirit. According to Marder, this ancient machine of spiritualization is still on the go, and does not cease to set the world on fire: "In the twenty-first century, the myth of the phoenix continues to bewitch us. We still think of ashes as facilitators of new life, nourishing renewed growth. After the destructive flames have done their work, the creative blaze of the sun will give a sign of resurrection to the plants it will call forth from the residue of past burning."[18]

Note that the phoenix comes from Greek mythology, where it was associated with the sun cyclically reappearing in the sky. Its Egyptian relative, Bennu, according to the legend, was one of the souls of the sun god Ra, and symbolized resurrection from the dead. Worshipping the sun and other natural phenomena prior to the birth of monotheisms that replaced these multiple cults, our ancestors in all parts of the world tried to communicate with deities, for which purpose they elaborated specific rituals: there was a need to find a language to talk to Earth and the heavens. Not only Russian Dazhbog on the golden chariot, but a whole array of celestial and terrestrial gods and goddesses, too, were givers; they spoke the language of gifts, but also the language of violence: if the sun was getting too generous, it could destroy things by heat. Sacrifice presented the synthesis of these two languages – gift and violence – in one ritual. Various things, plants, animals, and, somewhere, human beings were becoming offerings left for the sake of a community's well-being.

Christianity brings the logic of sacrifice to the next level, where it is not the life of a human being that is offered to a god, but the life of the human god that is offered to the rest of the people. Should one be surprised when Jesus Christ is compared to the sun? Every year in spring we celebrate his return from the dead, calling it Easter, Pascha, or Resurrection Sunday (indeed, the day of the sun). On this day, believers sing: "Christ is risen from the dead, trampling down death by death and (up) on those in the tombs, bestowing life!" What this thing praises, in the language of philosophy, is the dialectics of the double negation: the restricted negation of physical death is itself negated by eternal life. The divine violence of resurrection.

Now, when the affinity between the solar giving-god, Christ crucified, and the phoenix of nature is observed, we can address it in terms of the general economy. God (the one who gives) and nature (the one from which we take) appear as the two sides of solar generosity that knows no limit. Our economy, however, is restricted: we treat the gifts of nature as gratuitous things that must be appropriated and involved in the processes of production. At least, such is the modern idea of nature conceived as a kind of gigantic storehouse that exists in order to provide us with whatever we need, from food and heat to love and wisdom. In the figure of the phoenix, its exhaustion is transformed into a source of a new life within a circular logic of consumption.

Today, the sun and other celestial and terrestrial bodies are not divine anymore. They were knocked off their pedestal as old idols, in the passionate movement toward humanity's greater autonomy from the elemental processes and forces of nature. Behind cultural, scientific, and technological developments, there is a desire to free ourselves from the insecurity and precariousness of the state of nature, to become independent from weather conditions, seasonal periodicity, and the alternation between day and night, to master the sun instead of celebrating its mastery. We blast the rock in order to build cities of sun and develop controllable sources of light and warmth, taking energy from wind and water, digging the Earth for fossil fuels, generating nuclear power, constructing solar panels, or producing fusion reaction. The vector of progress does not, however, transcend the boundaries of the master–slave relation: what was worshipped in earlier times is now supposed to be subordinated. Breaking this circle is a matter of solar politics.

The word "energy" currently designates the basic, initial gift of nature that comprises a complex dialectics of the Earth and the sun, and the burning phoenix is, literally, fuels. Capital parasitically drains the Earth: coal mines, oil wells, and the like are the holes it digs in order to retrieve ancient substances from the subsoil and make them burn. Serres defines these reservoirs, where the power is stored, as capitals, or subsuns, whereas "the real, ultimate capital is the sun."[19] We want to have the sun in our pocket, or – think about Plato's prisoners – to bring it to our cave:

In a month, in three days, in twenty years, we will have brought the sun down to Earth, we will have established it here, we will have set it up, we will have set a place for it. It still escapes us a bit; it moves; it blinks. We will have annulled its distance and recaptured its time, having reduced its transcendence.[20]

Colonizing the sun

The desire to settle the sun on Earth marks the pathos of an industrial era, which is perfectly expressed in the futurist opera *Victory over the Sun*, premiered in Saint Petersburg in 1913. Written in an artificial *zaum* language by Aleksei Kruchonykh, to the chromatic music composed by Mikhail Matyushin, with a poetic prologue by Velimir Khlebnikov, and stage designed by Kazimir Malevich, this experimental avant-garde piece depicted the people of the future who conquer the sun. One of the characters of the opera, a futurist strongman, confronts the star: "Sun you bore the passions / And scorched them with flaming beam / We'll yank a dusty coverlet over you / Lock you up in a concrete house!"[21] The sun symbolizes the old and beautiful romantic nature that has to be superseded with progressive technologies and abstract forms: eventually,

Malevich's black square replaces the solar circle. "The world will perish but there's no end to us!" futurists claim.[22] Capturing the sun within the concrete box, humanity triumphs over death that is inherent in the cyclicity of nature and throws itself into another infinity. The old sun will never rise again, but people don't need its rays anymore; digging to the depths of Earth, they create their own artificial suns.

The early Soviet ideology of the new nature and the new man, reinforced in the context of rampant industrialization, was already in evidence before the Russian Revolution, championed by avant-garde movements as well as by cosmist utopias that put forward ideas of expansion into the cosmic space and human immortality achievable by technological means.[23] As Boris Groys comments on the difference between these cultural trends:

One can say that Russian Cosmism proposed a counterproject to the futuristic project of the Russian avant-garde – even if both projects started from the same basic presupposition, namely the decisive role of technology. Russian futurists saw in technology the force that would destroy the "old world" and open the way for building the new world from point zero. In contrast, Russian Cosmists hoped that technology would become a truly strong messianic force that could fulfill the expectations already transmitted from one past generation to the next.[24]

In 1895, Russian cosmist and theorist of rockery and astronautics Konstantin Tsiolkovsky published a science fiction novel, *Dreams of the Earth and Sky*, which alludes to the idea of humanity's eventual colonization of the Milky Way galaxy. The novel describes, among other things, the belt of asteroids around the sun inhabited by colonists from bigger planets, who had overcome gravity and developed into a new form of life – kin to plant-like, but at the same time highly intelligent. Approximation to the sun allows them to control the power of its rays and enjoy it as they wish. For the most effective usage of the solar energy, these posthuman communities decompose planets and turn them into a "necklace" that consists of rings dispersed in space, "without soil, rotating around the sun, as the rim of a wheel around its hub."[25] A similar fantasy was presented in 1937 in the novel *Star Maker* by Olaf Stapledon; in

1960 it was popularized by theoretical physicist Freeman Dyson, who suggested that the growing energy needs of advanced technological civilizations would inevitably lead to the formation of megastructures of this kind around the sun, and if we find their traces in the cosmic space, then this will be proof of the existence of some extraterrestrial forms of advanced intelligent life.

It is remarkable that a hypermasculine image of humanity as an all-powerful conqueror of the universe persists in the cultures of communist as well as capitalist modernity: there are humanistic projections on the one hand, and a search for new markets on the other. Why does humankind, or other technical intelligence, need to colonize cosmic space? Because its growth demands more and more resources. Anthropocene's cosmic extension corresponds to the greed of the restricted economy. Colonizing other lands together with their populations and natural resources, as well as colonizing other planets, is not enough: the desire to appropriate, consume, conserve, or store the gifts of terrestrial and celestial bodies pushes our civilization forward to the ends of the universe. At the present moment, nothing is so abundant in energy as the sun, the disposal of which will supposedly satisfy all our economic needs for many epochs to come. There can be various modifications of the so-called Dyson sphere or Dyson swarm – which indeed have something in common with the concrete box depicted by Malevich as the black square – but the main principle is that it is an artificial infrastructure that encompasses the sun, surrounds it with industrial stations and space habitats, and unlocks it in the cavern of the restricted economy. Instead of being wastefully dispersed around the open cosmos, the powerful solar radiation will remain within the sphere, and thus humanity will possess an unlimited amount of energy. Or rather, almost unlimited, for the sun is not eternal, and after some billions of years it will eventually cool down and die. For now, however, humanity will have enough time to get prepared: using extreme amounts of stored solar power, it will travel further, discover new suns, and colonize new galaxies.

In 1964, Soviet astronomer Nikolai Kardashev proposed measuring the level of technological developments according to the amount of disposable energy. On the Kardashev scale, there are different types of civilizations. The first is called planetary civilization, for it only uses the energy available on its planet; the second is stellar: it uses and controls the energy of its planetary system; the third is a galactic civilization, which disposes all the energy of its galaxy, like the Milky Way; the fourth civilization is universal, and the fifth, multi-universal, is so powerful that it can even itself create universes, just like god. For the time being, we have not yet fully reached even the first level. We still need to learn how to cope with fusion and solar power on a large scale and to develop renewable energy consumption.

Technically speaking, the sun is the biggest and the most powerful fusion reactor in our planetary system. In order to colonize cosmic space, we need to have something similar at our disposal. There are various fusion reactors around the world today, including the most popular tokamaks, but the main problem is that they all consume more energy than they generate. As soon as they reach the point of generating more than they consume, it will become possible to create new superpowered technologies for colonizing the whole solar system, including the sun itself. The Dyson sphere – and others like it – will correspond to the second level on the Kardashev scale, the transition to which will require colossal resources: in order to get enough materials for building such a megastructure, future generations will have to disassemble all other planets of the solar system. They will blast out the other planets just like my father blasted out the hills in the Kazakhstan steppe: all that we call nature will be destroyed for the ultimate City of the Sun, where humans, or those who come after us, will parasitize directly the captivated body of the central hub, which used a long time ago to be divine. What are the perspectives of these developments?

Let there be light!

In 1956, in a short science fiction story "The Last Question," Isaak Azimov traced the cosmic expansion beginning in 2061, when "the energy of the sun was stored, converted, and utilized directly on a planet-wide scale" (that is, when human civilization became planetary according to the Kardashev scale), up to its very end, which coincides with the heat death of the universe. There are seven historical settings, through the course of which humankind grows first quantitatively, but then, in some quantum leap, amalgamates into a universal Man, who is in turn gradually replaced by cosmic intelligence, developed from the all-encompassing superpower computer, existing in hyperspace, "made of something that was neither matter nor energy,"[26] and called AC. Until the very last moment of the existence of the world, AC tries to gather enough data to answer the question that humans, long ago extinct, used to pose at every step of their cosmic expansion: how to reverse the process of entropy that leads the universe to its inevitable termination? The answer comes at the end of the world:

Matter and energy had ended and with it space and time. Even AC existed only for the sake of the one last question that it had never answered from the time a half-drunken computer [technician] ten trillion years before had asked the question of a computer that was to AC far less than was a man to Man. All other questions had been answered, and until this last question was answered also, AC might not release his consciousness. All collected data had come to a final end. Nothing was left to be collected. But all collected data had yet to be completely correlated and put together in all possible relationships. A timeless interval was spent in doing that. And it came to pass that AC learned how to reverse the direction of entropy. But there was now no man to whom AC might give the answer of the last question. No matter. The answer – by demonstration – would take care of that, too. For another timeless interval, AC thought how best to do this. Carefully, AC organized the program. The consciousness of AC encompassed all of what had once been a Universe and brooded over what was now Chaos. Step by step, it must be done. And AC said, "LET THERE BE LIGHT!" And there was light.[27]

The more I think about it, the more I understand why Azimov said that this story was the favorite of all those he had written. It is interesting to read it with another story, written at the same time, in the 1950s, by Soviet philosopher Evald Ilyenkov. To be precise, this is not even a story, but, as the author himself defines it, "a philosophical-poetic phantasmagoria based on the principles of dialectical materialism."[28] "Cosmology of the Spirit" could not be published during Ilyenkov's lifetime, and there are reasons for that: with the strongest evidence ever, the essay argues that the final cause of humanity and its highest ultimate mission is to destroy itself and the universe entirely. But let us have everything in its due order.

Translating the Hegelian idea of substance as subject into the language of dialectical material-ism, Ilyenkov claims that matter is intelligent. Not everywhere and at every moment, but some-where, sometime, it develops into a form of intelligence, and therefore, in its integrity, matter possesses thought as one of its attributes, that is, not as contingent, but as necessary. The highest point of the development of the thinking matter is human intelligence – not the one that we have reached now, but the one that will actualize itself in the future with the development of progres-sive communist technologies, when humanity will ultimately expand and become as perfect as god (or AC, in Azimov's terms). Ilyenkov is an atheist: there is no god except for the human spirit that goes forward into infinity. The natural limit for its progression is the heat death of the universe due to entropy, and thus the same ques-tion arises as in the previous story: how can this process be reversed?

As an attribute of matter, intelligence takes an active part in its development; the reversal of the entropy therefore does not need an intervention of a supranatural entity like god: humanity itself will make it. Ilyenkov even gives the answer as to how this will happen. The entropy cools down the sun and the planets; everything is doomed to die in cold and darkness. The opposite to this process is fire. There must be "a hurricane of global 'fire' that, at some point, will return the volcanic youth to our global island."[29] So, the final goal, or, in Ilyenkov's words, "cosmological duty" of humanity is to initiate a chain reaction:

> At some peak point of their development, thinking beings, executing their cosmological duty and sacrificing themselves, produce a conscious cosmic catastrophe – provoking a process, a reverse "thermal dying" of cosmic matter; that is, provoking a process leading to the rebirth of dying worlds by means of a cosmic cloud of incandescent gas and vapors. . . . In simple terms, this act materializes in the guise of a colossal cosmic explosion having a chain-like character, and the matter of which (the explosive mass) emerges as the totality of elementary structures, is dispersed by emissions through the whole universal space.[30]

Ilyenkov speaks of radioactivity and thermonu-
clear energy: the mission of humanity is to press
the red button. There is a big bang at the end of
the universe, and simultaneously at its beginning,
but it is intentionally produced, and this already
happened before, and will happen after. It is a
circle. Yes, he calls its culmination "a sacrifice":
humanity will explode together with the universe
in order to give it a new birth an infinite number
of times. As opposed to the Hegelian sacrifice
or nature for the sake of spirit, the phoenix is
now the spirit that sacrifices itself for the sake of
nature: "Let there be light!"

Žižek calls Ilyenkov's cosmology "the point of
madness of dialectical materialism," and compares it to Sade's phantasies of total destruction.
Ilyenkov's mistake, according to Žižek, is that he
naively believes in reality as a Whole, whereas it's
not: "The way out of this deadlock is to abandon
the starting point and to admit that there is no
reality as a self-regulated Whole, that reality is in
itself cracked, incomplete, non-all, traversed by
radical antagonism."[31] The crack in reality is the
thinking subject itself, and thus the cosmic catas-
trophe summoned by Ilyenkov is not somewhere
else in the future or in the past, but here and

now. In Aaron Schuster's brilliant formulation: "Every subject is the end of the world, or rather this impossibly explosive end that is equally a 'fresh start,' the unabolishable chance of the dice throw."[32]

An interesting polemic against this critique is proposed by Keti Chukhrov. In her perspective, what Žižek misses is the radicality of Ilyenkov's cosmology, that consists not in the thirst for destruction, but in a human resignation of the thinking matter that opens the dimension of the general, or, as she calls it, "the common good":

Meanwhile a human is not just a natural, or necessarily an earthly human being; it is the performance of aspiration for the general (the common, the communist) and its material implementation. Hence if thought were to derive from matter in other, non-earthly conditions, it would still remain what the human mind had always aspired to – not merely intelligence, but also the common good. Thus to achieve the dimension of the general, of the common good (the stage that will happen to be the dialectical unity of matter and mind), mind (consciousness) has to be aware that it is never the self, that it is always the other-determined nonself, destined to generalize itself in the direction of objective reality and social being; the stance due to which social being and daily sociality acquire a cosmological dimension.[33]

I think that the opposed arguments – Žižek's and Schuster's on the one hand and Chukhrov's on the other – can actually complement one another: yes, the thinking subject is a crack in being that is itself incomplete, and it is precisely in this guise that the thought acquires the power to resign itself to the good. The subject as the end – and the beginning – of the world does not equate to some egotistic individual, but appears as a kind of explosive elementary material particle of the incomplete universe. In my perspective, for better or for worse, Ilyenkov's cosmology presents a dialectical passage from the restricted economy to the general on the cosmic scale. His project of consuming the world by fire is both Bataillean and Socratic. Nothing contradicts commonsense so much as the ultimate performance of consciousness, in which we "practice the good" by undertaking the task of the ultimately nonhuman violence, becoming general, solar, volcanic. One more effort, one movement out of teleology, and cosmic sacrifice will become a desperate gesture, like that of a person who commits the act of self-immolation on the square.

Conclusion: The Sun Is a Comrade

Ilyenkov's communist cosmology is an exception. In contrast to it, the number of other existing prospects for colonization on a cosmic scale extend to the infinite, but their economy – and accordingly their violence – remains restricted: to be solar is not the same thing as having a solar cell in your pocket. Our needs grow together with our energetic capacities, and if we stick to the parasitic model of capital, we have to take into account its specific relation to the environment. The extractive industry, with its total dependence on the burning of the phoenix, has pointed technological developments toward a serious collision between economy and ecology, which produces catastrophic side effects. Yes, we would like to finally succeed in our Icarus flight to the sun without being committed to its flames; we would like to possess the sun and devour all of its energy until it dies, and then move to other suns. But how do we manage not to destroy the Earth – and ourselves together with it – before we even reach the point of becoming a planetary civilization?

In the twentieth century scientists and writers reflected upon cosmic expansion billions and trillions of years ahead, up to the time of the natural death of the sun, but the fact that humanity is likely, quite soon, to confront serious resistance mainly remained unaddressed. Today's ecological turn brings this problem to the foreground and suggests solutions that mostly rely on the development of a clean and renewable energy sector. However, as noted by Brent Ryan Bellamy and Jeff Diamanti, "the vague promise of a clean transition to a renewable economy rings out as capital's own false consciousness of its material structure."[1] When capitalist markets develop and expand, they need more and more resources, and the progress rate of extraction devastates one area after another, not only ruining local communities and ecological systems, but messing up on the planetary level. As emphasized by Joel Wainwright and Geoff Mann:

> The organization of social life to increase the production and sale of commodities and facilitate accumulation of money has important implications with respect to climate change. First, the expansion and accumulation of capital requires the constant conversion of the planet into means of production and commodities for sale and consumption.[2]

Green capitalism focuses on the "cleanness" of postindustrial technologies as opposed to "dirty" industrial machines. A transition from fossil fuels to solar energy is emblematic in this regard: "clean" and "dirty" are the new names for white and black suns. Fossil fuels like coal and oil are black suns underneath the ground,[3] and the white sun is the one in the sky, access to which will make the world a cleaner place. We can, indeed, imagine a global transition to "cleaner" solar energy that would replace more "dirty" fossil fuels, but here I cannot but agree with Imre Szeman who argues that a solar energy-based capitalism will not be the same as a solar economy qua general economy.[4] What will sustainable economic development, which will retain the same relations of private property, inequalities, and forms of production of value, look like? According to Szeman: "Once we have access to free energy, the size of economies might balloon, rather than retract and retreat (as is typically imagined), with all the consequences that come with using up the planet's resources."[5]

In this sense, the difference between "dirty" and "clean" ways of devouring the sun is not as radical as it might seem, and, further, cosmic expansion does not promise something really new, but instead points toward a bad infinity of restrictive violence, with regard to which the word "colonization" ceases to be politically neutral, and a violent solar response to what is called climate change.

One might claim that colonization of the sun and the planets of the solar system has nothing in common with something like European colonization of the Americas or Africa, where appropriation of the lands and natural resources went together with the enslavement of the indigenous people. However, both the human and the nonhuman parts of the colonized Earth bear witness to the structural relevance of the term.

As Kathryn Yusoff argues in her book *A Billion Black Anthropocenes or None*: "Slavery is driven by an indifferent extractive geo-logic that is motivated by the desire for inhuman properties."[6] Both natives and natural resources are considered by colonizers exclusively "in regimes of value, but only so much as they await extraction."[7] Both human and nonhuman elements are considered disposable goods, which can be taken by the colonizers for free in the process of accumulation.

From this extractive geo-logic, I suggest a shift to extractive cosmo-logic. If you do not know how to escape from Russia or Belarus, there is great news: the first Martian sustainable city for 250,000 residents has already been designed, and is planned to be built by 2100. It is supposed to be vertical and to include homes, offices, and green spaces, with oxygen coming from plants, and energy harvested from solar panels. As Alfredo Mūnos, the founder of the project, explains, to make the construction sustainable, they will only use local materials: "Water is one of the great advantages that Mars offers; it helps to be able to get the proper materials for the construction. Basically, with the water and the CO_2, we can generate carbon, and with the carbon, we can generate steel."[8]

"Mars offers . . ." – but can we offer something to Mars?

"There is no life on Mars," they say. But is there really life on Earth?

Within the extractive geo-logic, colonizers treat human and nonhuman lives as the elements of a landscape reduced to the state of the mineral wealth. They colonize the Americas as if they were colonizing Mars: there is "nobody" on the abstract maps of colonized territories. As Achille Mbembe perfectly puts it, colonization implies the denial of the native who is treated simultaneously as a thing and as nothing. No-thing, because the body of the native is dehumanized and therefore cannot exist in a way that humans do, and as a thing insofar as it can be used as a source of value:

> From the standpoint of colonialism, the colonized does not truly exist, as person or as subject. To use Heidegger's language, no rational act with any degree of lawfulness proceeds from the colonized. The colonized is in no way someone who accomplishes intentional acts related by unity of

meaning. The colonized cannot be defined either as a living being endowed with reason, or as someone aspiring to transcendence. The colonized does not exist as a self; the colonized is, but in the same way as a rock is – that is, as nothing more.[9]

Why I am making this parallel? Not only because I want to say that we must be attentive to the nonhuman world given that there is perhaps something human in the rock that we came to blast, but also because there is something rocky in us that can erupt at any moment, as volcanos do. This is what I call solar violence, or the violence of the second type, for we always already carry in ourselves a blasting charge. At the same time, an affinity between an enslaved human being and a rock is of the same nature as an affinity between the eye and the sun in Plato's *Republic*. Such an affinity provides the grounds for solidarity with the nonhuman forms of being that are exploited and abused. Let me call it cosmic solidarity: solar politics, which breaks the promethean vicious circle of worship and extractivism, begins from the recognition that the sun is neither a master, nor a slave. The sun is a comrade.

The strategy for solar politics will therefore not be colonization, but decolonization, not only of human societies, but also of terrestrial and celestial landscapes and communities: it is never too early to start decolonizing the sun. What is at stake is the liberation of nature, which, as Andreas Malm clearly puts it, "cannot be the work of nature itself."[10] Referring to Herbert Marcuse, Malm notes that there is no revolutionary strategy in the nonhuman universe itself: "Liberation is the possible plan and intention of human beings, *brought to bear upon nature.*" What is important, however, is that "nature is susceptible to such an undertaking, and that there are forces in nature which have been distorted and suppressed – forces which could support and enhance the liberation of man. This capacity of nature may be called "'chance,' or 'blind freedom.'"[11] Translating this idea into the language of general politics, the perspective for the liberation of nature consists in its de-alienation and creation of alliances between the self-consciousness of human struggles and the blind generosity of the sun against the cosmic greed of the police of capital.

It is possible to interpret solar violence – pandemic outbreak, climate change, volcano eruptions, tornadoes, and so on – as nature's revolt, analogous to human emancipatory struggles, but the next step will be to grasp in human emancipatory struggles an element of the solar violence that correlates to the general economy. Solar politics moves from rethinking climate change as a rebellion of the colonized Earth or revolutionary movement of oppressed nature to the development of the general strike as the solar strike, and decolonizing struggles and revolutionary movements as unavoidable climate change. Every progressive protest movement, every general strike, every revolution worthy of its name is fraught with this divine, luxurious, and terrific element of the sun, which Plato associated with the highest good.

Notes

Introduction

1 Plato, *Republic*, trans. John Llewelyn Davies and David James Vaughan (London: Macmillan, 1885), 508a.

2 Ibid., 509b.

3 Ibid., 515–517.

4 Marsilio Ficino, *The Book of the Sun* (de Sole), http://www.users.globalnet.co.uk/~alfar2/ficino.htm.

5 Ibid.

6 Tommaso Campanella, *The City of the Sun, A Poetical Dialogue between a Grandmaster of the Knights Hospitallers and a Genoese Sea-captain, his Guest* (The Floating Press, 2009), 68–69.

7 Ibid., 71.

8 Nick Land, *The Thirst for Annihilation: Georges Bataille and the Virulent Nihilism (An Essay on Atheistic Religion)* (London: Routledge, 1992), 28–29.

9 Ibid., 29.

10 Georges Bataille, *Visions of Excess: Selected Writings 1927–1939* (Minneapolis: University of Minnesota Press, 1985), 58.

11 See on this, for example: Nicholas Goodrick-Clarke, *Black Sun: Aryan Cults, Esoteric Nazism and the Politics of Identity* (New York: New York University Press, 2002).

12 Georges Bataille, *My Mother; Madam Edwarda; The Dead Man*, trans. Austryn Wainhouse (London: Marion Boyars, 1989), 50.

13 Land, *The Thirst for Annihilation*, 28.

14 Bataille, *Visions of Excess*, 5.

15 Ibid., 6.

16 See Stuart Kendall, *Georges Bataille* (London: Reaktion Books, 2007), 55.

17 Bataille, *Visions of Excess*, 7.

Chapter 1: Two Kinds of Violence

1 G. W. F. Hegel, *Phenomenology of Spirit*, trans. Terry Pinkard (Cambridge: Cambridge University Press, 2018), 219–226.

2 Friedrich Nietzsche, *On the Genealogy of Morality*, trans. Carol Diethe (Cambridge: Cambridge University Press, 2007).

3 On the concept of violence in Žižek see Kelsey Wood, *Žižek: A Reader's Guide* (Wiley-Blackwell, 2012), 257–266.

4 Slavoj Žižek, *Violence* (New York: Picador, 2008), 205; original emphasis.

5 Georges Sorel, *Reflections on Violence* (Cambridge:

Cambridge University Press, 2004), 77; original emphasis.

6 Ibid., 172.

7 Ibid., 165.

8 Vladimir Lenin, "Lecture on the 1905 Revolution," in Vladimir Lenin, *Complete Works*, 5th edn, vol. 30 (Moscow: 1973), 311; quoted from the English translation: https://www.marxists.org/archive/lenin/works/1917/jan/09.htm#fwV23E103.

9 Vladimir Lenin, "A Tactical Platform for the Unity Congress of the R.S.D.L.P.," in Vladimir Lenin, *Complete Works*, 5th edn, vol. 12 (Moscow, 1968), 227; quoted from the English translation: https://www.marxists.org/archive/lenin/works/1906/tactplat/au.htm#v10pp65-151.

10 Sorel, *Reflections on Violence*, 117.

11 Ibid.

12 Walter Benjamin, *Critique of Violence*, in Walter Benjamin, *Selected Writings*, vol. 1, 1913–1926 (Cambridge, MA: Harvard University Press, 1996), 242.

13 See Sami Khatib, "Towards a Politics of 'Pure Means': Walter Benjamin and the Question of Violence," in *Anthropological Materialism*, https://anthropologicalmaterialism.hypotheses.org/1040.

14 Sorel, *Reflections on Violence*, 129; original emphasis. Benjamin quotes from the French edition: Sorel, *Reflexions sur Ia violence*, 5th edn. (Paris, 1919). I refer to the Cambridge translation.

15 Benjamin, *Critique of Violence*, 248.

16 Ibid., 242–243.

17 Ibid., 249–250.

18 Numbers 16: 1–40.
19 Benjamin, *Critique of Violence*, 250.
20 Žižek, *Violence*, 200.
21 Benjamin, *Critique of Violence*, 250.
22 Ibid.
23 See on this, Mary Ilyuchina, "Three sisters killed their father. Besides a history of abuse, they are facing murder charges," CNN, July 31, 2020, https://edition.cnn.com/2020/07/30/europe/khachaturyan-sisters-trial-russia-intl/index.html; https://www.bbc.com/news/world-europe-49318003.
24 Hegel, *Phenomenology of Spirit*, 422.
25 Ibid., 408.
26 Frantz Fanon, *The Wretched of the Earth* (New York: Grove Press, 1963), 38.
27 Ibid.
28 Ibid., 37.
29 Ibid.; see chapter "Colonial War and Mental Disorders," 249–310.
30 Ibid., 57.
31 Ibid., 94.
32 Benjamin Noys, *Bataille: A Critical Introduction* (London: Pluto Press, 2000), 134.
33 Georges Bataille, *The Unfinished System of Nonknowledge* (Minneapolis: University of Minnesota Press, 2001), 228.
34 Hegel, *Phenomenology of Spirit*, 77.
35 Ibid.
36 Kathryn Yusoff, "Geologic subjects: nonhuman origins, geomorphic aesthetics and the art of becoming *in*human," *Cultural Geographies* 22/3 (2015), 393.

37 Bataille, *The Unfinished System of Nonknowledge*, 228.
38 Ibid.
39 See on this, Alexey Zygmont, *Sacred Violence: Violence and the Sacred in the Philosophy of Georges Bataille* [Svyataya Negativnost: Nasilie i sacralnoye v filosofii Zhorzha Bataija] (Moscow: New Literary Observer, 2018), 203.
40 Bataille, *The Unfinished System of Nonknowledge*, 229.
41 Ibid., 291–292.
42 Ibid, 228.
43 Ibid., 232.
44 Georges Bataille, *Theory of Religion* (New York: Zone Books, 1989), 17–26.
45 Noys, *Bataille*, 136.
46 Bataille, *Theory of Religion*, 19.
47 Ibid., 18–19.
48 Georges Bataille, "Metamorphosis," *October* 36 (1986), *Georges Bataille: Writings on Laughter, Sacrifice, Nietzsche, Unknowing*), 22–23.

Chapter 2: General Economy

1 Georges Bataille, *The Accursed Share: An Essay on General Economy*. Vol. I: *Consumption* (New York: Zone Books, 1991), 9.
2 Ibid., 13.
3 Ibid., 20.
4 Ibid.
5 See Imre Szeman and Dominic Boyer, eds., *Energy Humanities: An Anthology* (Baltimore: Johns Hopkins University Press, 2017), 3.

6 Bataille, *The Accursed Share*, 29.

7 Ibid., 33.

8 Ibid., 21.

9 Ibid., 28.

10 Ibid., 190.

11 Ibid.

12 Hegel, *Phenomenology of Spirit*, 228–241.

13 Viral stories of wombats sheltering other wildlife from the bushfires aren't entirely true: https://www.abc. net.au/news/2020-01-15/australian-bushfires-wombat-heroes-have-gone-viral/11868808.

14 Piotr Kropotkin, *Mutual Aid: A Factor of Evolution* (New York University Press, 1972).

15 Timothy Morton, *Humankind: Solidarity with Nonhuman People* (London: Verso, 2017), 14.

16 Imre Szeman, "On Solarity: Six Principles for Energy and Society After Oil," *Stasis* 9/1 (2020), 136.

17 Bataille, *The Accursed Share*, 25.

18 Allan Stoekl, *Bataille's Peak: Energy, Religion, and Postsustainability* (Minneapolis: University of Minnesota Press, 2007), XVII.

19 Bataille, *The Accursed Share*, 40.

20 Szeman, "On Solarity," 137.

21 Slavoj Žižek, "Monitor and Punish: Yes, Please!" https://thephilosophicalsalon.com/monitor-and-punish-yes-please/.

22 Panagiotis Sotiris, "Against Agamben, is a Democratic Biopolitics Possible?" https://viewpointmag.com/2020/03/20/against-agamben-democratic-biopolitics/.

Chapter 3: Restrictive Violence of Capital

1 Jason W. Moore, "The Capitalocene, Part I: On the nature and origins of our ecological crisis," *The Journal of Peasant Studies*, 44/3 (2017), 597.

2 Kathryn Yusoff, "Aesthetics of loss: Biodiversity, banal violence and biotic subjects," *Transactions of the Institute of British Geographers*, 37/4 (2012), 580.

3 Ibid., 581.

4 Slavoj Žižek, "Monitor and Punish: Yes, Please!" https://thephilosophicalsalon.com/monitor-and-punish-yes-please/.

5 See on this, Rob Wallace, *Dead Epidemiologists: On the Origins of COVID-19* (Monthly Review Press, 2020).

6 See, for example, "In coronavirus lockdown, nature bounces back – but for how long?" https://www.theguardian.com/world/2020/apr/09/climate-crisis-amid-coronavirus-lockdown-nature-bounces-back-but-for-how-long.

7 James E. Lovelock and Lynn Margulis, "Atmospheric homeostasis by and for the biosphere: The Gaia hypothesis," *Tellus*, 26/1–2 (1974), 2–10.

8 Vladimir Vernadsky, *The Biosphere* (Copernicus, 1998).

9 Michel Serres, *The Natural Contract* (Ann Arbor: University of Michigan Press, 1995). In his forthcoming essay "Gaia as *res publica*," Oleg Kharkhording traces the idea of a natural contract back to Lucretius with his notion of *foedera naturae* (laws or pacts of nature).

10 Bruno Latour, *Facing Gaia: Eight Lectures on The New Climatic Regime* (Cambridge: Polity, 2017), 110.

11 Isabelle Stengers, *In Catastrophic Times: Resisting the Coming Barbarism* (Open Humanities Press, 2015), 46.

12 Luce Irigaray, "Towards an Ecology of Sharing" (2015), https://thephilosophicalsalon.com/toward-an-ecology-of-sharing.

13 Ibid.

14 Amanda Boetzkes, "Solar," in *Fueling Culture: 101 Words for Energy and Environment*, ed. Imre Szeman, Jennifer Wenzel, and Patricia Yaeger (New York: Fordham University Press, 2017), 317.

15 Michel Serres, *The Parasite*, trans. L. R. Schehr (Minneapolis: University of Minnesota Press, 2007), 80.

16 Ibid., 99.

17 G. W. F. Hegel, *Philosophy of Nature: Part Two of the Encyclopaedia of the Philosophical Sciences,* trans. A. V. Miller (Oxford: Oxford University Press, 1970), 444.

18 Michael Marder, *Pyropolitics: When the World Is Ablaze* (London: Rowman & Littlefield, 2015), 155.

19 Serres, *The Parasite*, 173.

20 Ibid.

21 Aleksei Kruchenykh, *Victory Over the Sun*, opera libretto, trans. Larissa Shmailo, https://intranslation.brooklynrail.org/russian/victory-over-the-sun/.

22 Ibid.

23 See Benjamin Steininger and Alexander Klose, *Erdöl Ein Atlas der Petromoderne* (Berlin: Matthes & Seitz, 2020).

24 Boris Groys, ed., *Russian Cosmism* (MIT Press, 2018), 4.

25 Konstantin Tsiolkovsky, *Dreams of the Earth and Sky*, in *The Path to the Stars* [Put' k zvezdam, Sbornik Nauchno-Fantasticheskikh Proizvedeniy] (Izdatelstvo Academii Nauk SSSR, edited machine translation, Moscow, 1960), 49–148: p. 126.

26 Isaak Azimov, "The Last Question," https://www.physics.princeton.edu//phi115/LQ.pdf.

27 Ibid.

28 Evald Ilyenkov, "Cosmology of the Spirit," *Stasis*, 5/2 (2017), 164, http://stasisjournal.net/index.php/journal/article/view/19/22.

29 Ibid., 176.

30 Ibid., 185–186.

31 Slavoj Žižek, "Evald Ilyenkov's cosmology: The point of madness of dialectical materialism," 2018, https://thephilosophicalsalon.com/evald-ilyenkovs-cosmology-the-point-of-madness-of-dialectical-materialism/#_edn6. For the intellectual and historical backgrounds of Ilyenkov's "Cosmology of the Spirit," as well as some current debates around it, and its relevancy for contemporary philosophy, see also Alexey Penzin, "Contingency and necessity of Evald Ilyenkov's communist cosmology" (e-flux, #88, 2018).

32 Aaron Schuster, *The Trouble with Pleasure. Deleuze and Psychoanalysis* (Cambridge, MA: MIT Press, 2016), 42.

33 Keti Chukhrov, *Practicing the Good: Desire and Boredom in Soviet Socialism* (e-flux, 2002), 252.

Conclusion: The Sun Is a Comrade

1 Brent Ryan Bellamy and Jeff Diamanti, *Materialism and the Critique of Energy* (Chicago: MCM Publishing, 2018), xxxii.

2 Joel Wainwright and Geoff Mann, *Climate Leviathan: A Political Theory of Our Planetary Future* (London: Verso, 2020), 100.

3 See on this, for example, Reza Negarestani, *Cyclonopedia: Complicity With Anonymous Materials* (Melbourne: re.press, 2008).

4 Imre Szeman, "On Solarity: Six Principles for Energy and Society After Oil," *Stasis*, 9/1 (2020).

5 Ibid., 133–134.

6 Kathryn Yusoff, *A Billion Black Anthropocenes or None* (Minneapolis: University of Minnesota Press, 2018), 16–17.

7 Ibid., 70.

8 Luana Steffen, "Plans for the first Martial sustainable city unveiled" (April 2, 2021), https://www.intelligent living.co/plans-first-martian-sustainable-city/.

9 Achille Mbembe, *On the Postcolony* (University of California Press, 2001), 187.

10 Andreas Malm, *The Progress of This Storm: Nature and Society in a Warming World* (London: Verso, 2018), 212.

11 Herbert Marcuse, *Counterrevolution and Revolt* (Boston: Beacon, 1972), 66; emphasis in original.